THIS BOOK BELONGS TO:

_____

_____

_____

JOURNAL # _____

DATES: /   /   —   /   /

DAILY JOURNAL

A DAILY JOURNAL FOR LAW ENFORCEMENT

© 2024 CHAD W FARLEY ALL RIGHTS RESERVED
UNAUTHORIZED REPRODUCTION OF THIS WORK
IS STRICTLY PROHIBITED.

DISCLAIMER: THIS JOURNAL IS INTENDED TO SERVE AS A TOOL TO ENCOURAGE MINDFULNESS, RESILIENCE, AND THE TRACKING OF DAILY HABITS RELATED TO MENTAL AND PHYSICAL HEALTH. IT IS NOT A SUBSTITUTE FOR PROFESSIONAL MEDICAL ADVICE, DIAGNOSIS, OR TREATMENT. ANY FITNESS, DIETARY, OR MENTAL HEALTH DECISIONS SHOULD BE MADE IN CONSULTATION WITH YOUR HEALTHCARE PROVIDER. THE USE OF THIS JOURNAL DOES NOT ESTABLISH A DOCTOR-PATIENT RELATIONSHIP.

THE CONTENT PROVIDED IN THIS JOURNAL IS FOR INFORMATIONAL PURPOSES ONLY AND IS NOT INTENDED TO REPLACE OR BE A SUBSTITUTE FOR PROFESSIONAL MEDICAL ADVICE, DIAGNOSIS, OR TREATMENT. ALWAYS SEEK THE ADVICE OF YOUR PHYSICIAN OR OTHER QUALIFIED HEALTH PROVIDER WITH ANY QUESTIONS YOU MAY HAVE REGARDING A MEDICAL CONDITION. NEVER DISREGARD PROFESSIONAL MEDICAL ADVICE OR DELAY IN SEEKING IT BECAUSE OF SOMETHING YOU HAVE READ IN THIS JOURNAL.

WHILE EVERY EFFORT HAS BEEN MADE TO ENSURE THE ACCURACY OF THE INFORMATION IN THIS JOURNAL, THE AUTHOR AND PUBLISHER EXPRESSLY DISCLAIM RESPONSIBILITY FOR ANY ERRORS OR OMISSIONS. NEITHER THE AUTHOR NOR THE PUBLISHER WILL BE HELD LIABLE OR RESPONSIBLE FOR ANY DAMAGE OR HARM YOU MAY SUFFER AS A RESULT OF FAILING TO SEEK COMPETENT MEDICAL OR HEALTH ADVICE FROM A PROFESSIONAL WHO IS FAMILIAR WITH YOUR SITUATION.

REMEMBER, THE JOURNEY TO HEALTH AND WELLNESS IS PERSONAL AND INDIVIDUAL. RESULTS AND PROGRESS WILL VARY FROM PERSON TO PERSON. THIS JOURNAL IS SIMPLY A TOOL TO DOCUMENT YOUR JOURNEY AND DOES NOT GUARANTEE ANY SPECIFIC OUTCOMES.

WELCOME TO THE DAILY JOURNAL

The Daily Journal is designed for simplicity, serving as a tool for mindfulness and gratitude to help restore and maintain a balanced and fulfilled life. This journal is tailored for police officers; regular men and women who are dedicated to their roles amidst immense pressure and challenges. The straightforward format of the journal aims to provide a practical and effective means of reflection and self-care, supporting officers in their daily routines and well-being. Each journal is designed to take six-months to complete. This interval will allow you the opportunity to graduate forward to subsequent journals, reestablishing a baseline, setting new goals, and embracing a new intention.

Today's Journal Pages

Each "Today's Journal" page is structured to capture essential aspects of your day, including:

Date and Day of the Week: Start by noting the date and marking the day of the week to ground yourself in the present.

Gratitude: Reflect on and list three things you are grateful for. Practicing gratitude can help maintain a positive outlook, even during challenging times.

Hydration: Use the scale to track your water intake throughout the day, ensuring you stay hydrated during your shift. Experts recommend around 100 ounces per day for active people. More if it's hot.

Exercise: Document the type and duration of your physical activity. Staying active is crucial for both physical and mental well-being. Just circle the type of exercise.

(Resistance,   Cardio,   Sports,   Yoga-Pilates,   Martial Arts)

Mood Scale: Assess and record your mood to increase self-awareness and monitor any patterns over time.

Reflection: Take a moment to jot down what went right during your day and what you learned from the experiences. Was there a particularly difficult call? Is organizational stress becoming overwhelming and interfering with your job satisfaction, or your ability to do it effectively?

Planning for Tomorrow: Use this section to prepare for the next day, setting intentions and identifying any potential challenges.

Weekly Planner Page

The weekly planner provides an overview of the week, allowing you to schedule tasks and commitments for each day. The small notes section offers space for any additional reminders or thoughts.

End of Week Reflection

As the week draws to a close, take time to process your experiences. The "notes" section enables you to capture any important details, while the "what I need to process" section encourages you to identify and address any lingering thoughts or emotions. By engaging with each section of this journal, you can cultivate a proactive and balanced approach to your well-being, both on and off duty. Embrace this opportunity for self-care and personal growth as you navigate the demands of your role.

Processing Lingering Thoughts and Emotions

The "What Do I Need to Process" section of your journal is a dedicated space for you to address and manage lingering thoughts and emotions. Here are some suggestions on how to effectively use this section:

Identify Your Emotions: Start by identifying what you're feeling. This could be stress, frustration, sadness, or any other emotion. Acknowledging your emotions is the first step towards processing them.

Understand the Cause: Reflect on what event or situation initiated these emotions. Understanding the cause can help you manage similar situations in the future.

Express Without Censoring: Write freely about your feelings without censoring yourself. This can help you gain a deeper understanding of your emotions and can be a form of emotional release.

Reflect on Your Thoughts and Reactions: Consider how you reacted to the situation and what thoughts you had. This can help you identify patterns in your behavior and reactions.

Consider Alternative Responses: Think about how you could have reacted differently. This can help you develop new strategies for managing similar situations in the future.

Plan for the Future: Based on your reflections, create a plan for how you can respond to similar situations in the future. This could involve developing new coping strategies or ways of thinking.

Practice Mindfulness: Mindfulness can help you stay present and focused, reducing the impact of negative thoughts and emotions. Consider incorporating mindfulness practices into your daily routine.

Seek Support When Needed: If you find that your thoughts and emotions are overwhelming or affecting your daily life, consider seeking support from the department Peer Support Team, a chaplain, or a mental health professional.

Remember, it's okay to have negative emotions. The goal is not to eliminate these emotions, but to understand and manage them in a healthy way. This section of your journal is a tool to help you do that. If the practice becomes too overwhelming or burdensome, please reach out to a professional therapist for help.

TODAY'S Journal

DOCUMENT WEATHER

DATE: 3 / 19 / 24

S M (T) W T F S

TODAY I'M GRATEFUL FOR:

1. TODAY I
2. MY PART
3. IT WAS N

> BE CREATIVE, BE HONEST.
> EVERY DAY CAN BE FILLED WITH GRATITUDE
> IF YOU LOOK DEEPLY ENOUGH.
> WHO DID YOU HELP? THAT'S WHY YOU GOT
> INTO THIS JOB TO BEGIN WITH ANYWAY.

WATER INTAKE
A GLASS = 12 OZ.

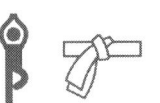

1 2 3 4 5 6 7 8 (Glass)

EXERCISE
(45) TIME

3MI. RUN/WALK

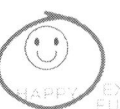

MOOD
ANGRY/FRUSTRATED · SAD · TIRED · NUMB · (HAPPY) · EXCITED/FULFILLED

WHAT WENT RIGHT

> DOCUMENT GOOD DECISIONS, TACTICAL SUCCESSES, CO-WORKERS YOU HELPED, EVENTS YOU ARE PROUD OF, ETC.

WHAT DID I LEARN

> LESSONS LEARNED, NEW TECHNIQUES, NEW LAWS, EVEN WHAT YOU LEARNED THE HARD WAY (MISTAKES)

FOR TOMORROW

> WHAT CAN YOU CONCENTRATE ON TOMORROW? WHAT DO YOU LOOK FORWAD TO? WHAT DO YOU NEED TO GET READY FOR?

WEEKLY *Planner*

MONDAY

- [x] CALL MOM & DAD
- [x] GET THE WIFE A CARD
- [ ] DO RANGE QUAL
- [ ] STOP BY BIKE RODEO AT THE ELEMENTARY SCHOOL

TUESDAY

NOTE UPCOMING APPOINTMENTS, TRAINING, SPECIAL EVENTS, OR GOALS FOR THE WEEK

WEDNESDAY

THURSDAY

FRIDAY

SATURDAY

SUNDAY

NOTES

USE THE NOTES SECTION TO IDENTIFY SPECIAL MOMENTS ABOUT THE WEEK, OR CARRY OVER THEMES FROM LAST WEEK

Check-in

Use this section to "check-in" with yourself. Take a moment to reflect on your current state of mind, emotions, and overall well-being. By establishing this baseline, you'll be able to look back and gauge your progress over time. Consider the following prompts for your check-in: How are you feeling today? What is on your mind? Are there any specific emotions or concerns you'd like to address? What are you grateful for in this moment?

Goal To Go

This section provides an opportunity for you to articulate your aspirations and intentions. Take a moment to consider what you hope to achieve through the journaling process. Reflect on specific areas of your life or work that you'd like to focus on, and envision your ideal future. By documenting your goals, you can lay the groundwork for a purposeful and fulfilling journaling journey.

WEEKLY *Planner*

MONDAY

TUESDAY

WEDNESDAY

THURSDAY

FRIDAY

SATURDAY

SUNDAY

NOTES

TODAY'S
Journal

DATE: / /

S M T W T F S

TODAY I'M GRATEFUL FOR:

1.
2.
3.

WATER INTAKE

1 2 3 4 5 6 7 8 (Glass)

EXERCISE

( ) TIME

MOOD

ANGRY/FRUSTRATED   SAD   TIRED   NUMB   HAPPY   EXCITED/FULFILLED

WHAT WENT RIGHT

WHAT DID I LEARN

FOR TOMORROW

TODAY'S Journal

DATE: / /

☼ ☼ ☼ ☼ ☼ ☼ ☼
S M T W T F S

TODAY I'M GRATEFUL FOR:

1. ....

2. ....

3. ....

WATER INTAKE

💧 💧 💧 💧 💧 💧 💧 💧
1 2 3 4 5 6 7 8 (Glass)

EXERCISE

( ) TIME

MOOD

ANGRY/FRUSTRATED SAD TIRED NUMB HAPPY EXCITED/FULFILLED

WHAT WENT RIGHT

....
....
....
....
....

WHAT DID I LEARN

....
....
....
....

FOR TOMORROW

....
....
....
....

TODAY'S Journal

DATE: / /

S M T W T F S

TODAY I'M GRATEFUL FOR:

1.

2.

3.

WATER INTAKE

1 2 3 4 5 6 7 8 (Glass)

EXERCISE

TIME

MOOD

ANGRY/FRUSTRATED SAD TIRED NUMB HAPPY EXCITED/FULFILLED

WHAT WENT RIGHT

WHAT DID I LEARN

FOR TOMORROW

TODAY'S Journal

DATE: / /

S M T W T F S

TODAY I'M GRATEFUL FOR:

1.
2.
3.

WATER INTAKE

1 2 3 4 5 6 7 8 (Glass)

EXERCISE

( ) TIME

MOOD

ANGRY/FRUSTRATED — SAD — TIRED — NUMB — HAPPY — EXCITED/FULFILLED

WHAT WENT RIGHT

WHAT DID I LEARN

FOR TOMORROW

TODAY'S
Journal

DATE: / /

S M T W T F S

TODAY I'M GRATEFUL FOR:

1.
2.
3.

WATER INTAKE

1 2 3 4 5 6 7 8 (Glass)

EXERCISE

(TIME)

MOOD

ANGRY/FRUSTRATED SAD TIRED NUMB HAPPY EXCITED/FULFILLED

WHAT WENT RIGHT

WHAT DID I LEARN

FOR TOMORROW

TODAY'S Journal

DATE: / /

S M T W T F S

TODAY I'M GRATEFUL FOR:

1.
2.
3.

WATER INTAKE

1 2 3 4 5 6 7 8 (Glass)

EXERCISE

( ) TIME

MOOD

ANGRY/FRUSTRATED SAD TIRED NUMB HAPPY EXCITED/FULFILLED

WHAT WENT RIGHT

WHAT DID I LEARN

FOR TOMORROW

TODAY'S Journal

DATE: ___ / ___ / ___

S M T W T F S

TODAY I'M GRATEFUL FOR:

1.
2.
3.

WATER INTAKE

1 2 3 4 5 6 7 8 (Glass)

EXERCISE

(_____) TIME

MOOD

ANGRY/FRUSTRATED · SAD · TIRED · NUMB · HAPPY · EXCITED/FULFILLED

WHAT WENT RIGHT

WHAT DID I LEARN

FOR TOMORROW

NOTES:

NOTES:

WHAT DO I NEED TO PROCESS:

WEEKLY *Planner*

MONDAY

TUESDAY

WEDNESDAY

THURSDAY

FRIDAY

SATURDAY

SUNDAY

NOTES

TODAY'S Journal

DATE: / /

S M T W T F S

TODAY I'M GRATEFUL FOR:

1.
2.
3.

WATER INTAKE

1 2 3 4 5 6 7 8 (Glass)

EXERCISE

( ) TIME

MOOD

ANGRY/FRUSTRATED SAD TIRED NUMB HAPPY EXCITED/FULFILLED

WHAT WENT RIGHT

WHAT DID I LEARN

FOR TOMORROW

TODAY'S Journal

DATE: / /

S M T W T F S

TODAY I'M GRATEFUL FOR:

1.
2.
3.

WATER INTAKE

1 2 3 4 5 6 7 8 (Glass)

EXERCISE

( ) TIME

MOOD

ANGRY/FRUSTRATED   SAD   TIRED   NUMB   HAPPY   EXCITED/FULFILLED

WHAT WENT RIGHT

WHAT DID I LEARN

FOR TOMORROW

TODAY'S Journal

DATE: / /

S M T W T F S

TODAY I'M GRATEFUL FOR:

1.
2.
3.

WATER INTAKE

1 2 3 4 5 6 7 8 (Glass)

EXERCISE

( )
TIME

MOOD

ANGRY/FRUSTRATED · SAD · TIRED · NUMB · HAPPY · EXCITED/FULFILLED

WHAT WENT RIGHT

WHAT DID I LEARN

FOR TOMORROW

TODAY'S Journal

DATE: / /

S M T W T F S

TODAY I'M GRATEFUL FOR:

1.

2.

3.

WATER INTAKE

1 2 3 4 5 6 7 8 (Glass)

EXERCISE

( ) TIME

MOOD

ANGRY/FRUSTRATED   SAD   TIRED   NUMB   HAPPY   EXCITED/FULFILLED

WHAT WENT RIGHT

WHAT DID I LEARN

FOR TOMORROW

TODAY'S Journal

DATE: / /

S M T W T F S

TODAY I'M GRATEFUL FOR:

1.
2.
3.

WATER INTAKE

1 2 3 4 5 6 7 8 (Glass)

EXERCISE

( ) TIME

MOOD

ANGRY/FRUSTRATED SAD TIRED NUMB HAPPY EXCITED/FULFILLED

WHAT WENT RIGHT

WHAT DID I LEARN

FOR TOMORROW

TODAY'S
Journal

DATE: /   /

S M T W T F S

TODAY I'M GRATEFUL FOR:

1.
2.
3.

WATER INTAKE

1 2 3 4 5 6 7 8 (Glass)

EXERCISE

( ) TIME

MOOD

ANGRY/FRUSTRATED   SAD   TIRED   NUMB   HAPPY   EXCITED/FULFILLED

WHAT WENT RIGHT

WHAT DID I LEARN

FOR TOMORROW

TODAY'S Journal

DATE: / /

S M T W T F S

TODAY I'M GRATEFUL FOR:

1. ....
2. ....
3. ....

WATER INTAKE

1 2 3 4 5 6 7 8 (Glass)

EXERCISE

( ) TIME

MOOD

ANGRY/FRUSTRATED SAD TIRED NUMB HAPPY EXCITED/FULFILLED

WHAT WENT RIGHT

WHAT DID I LEARN

FOR TOMORROW

NOTES:

NOTES:

WHAT DO I NEED TO PROCESS:

WEEKLY *Planner*

MONDAY

TUESDAY

WEDNESDAY

THURSDAY

FRIDAY

SATURDAY

SUNDAY

NOTES

TODAY'S
Journal

DATE: / /

S M T W T F S

TODAY I'M GRATEFUL FOR:

1. ....
2. ....
3. ....

WATER INTAKE

1 2 3 4 5 6 7 8 (Glass)

EXERCISE

( ) TIME

MOOD

ANGRY/FRUSTRATED   SAD   TIRED   NUMB   HAPPY   EXCITED/FULFILLED

WHAT WENT RIGHT

....
....
....
....
....

WHAT DID I LEARN

....
....
....

FOR TOMORROW

....
....
....

TODAY'S Journal

DATE: /   /

S M T W T F S

TODAY I'M GRATEFUL FOR:

1.
2.
3.

WATER INTAKE

1 2 3 4 5 6 7 8 (Glass)

EXERCISE

(   )
         TIME

MOOD

ANGRY/FRUSTRATED   SAD   TIRED   NUMB   HAPPY   EXCITED/FULFILLED

WHAT WENT RIGHT

WHAT DID I LEARN

FOR TOMORROW

TODAY'S Journal

DATE: / /

S M T W T F S

TODAY I'M GRATEFUL FOR:

1. ....
2. ....
3. ....

WATER INTAKE

1 2 3 4 5 6 7 8 (Glass)

EXERCISE

( )
TIME

MOOD

ANGRY/FRUSTRATED   SAD   TIRED   NUMB   HAPPY   EXCITED/FULFILLED

WHAT WENT RIGHT

WHAT DID I LEARN

FOR TOMORROW

TODAY'S Journal

DATE: / /

S M T W T F S

TODAY I'M GRATEFUL FOR:

1. ....
2. ....
3. ....

WATER INTAKE

1 2 3 4 5 6 7 8 (Glass)

EXERCISE

( ) TIME

MOOD

ANGRY/FRUSTRATED SAD TIRED NUMB HAPPY EXCITED/FULFILLED

WHAT WENT RIGHT

....
....
....
....
....

WHAT DID I LEARN

....
....
....
....

FOR TOMORROW

....
....
....
....

TODAY'S
Journal

DATE: / /

S M T W T F S

TODAY I'M GRATEFUL FOR:

1.
2.
3.

WATER INTAKE
1 2 3 4 5 6 7 8 (Glass)

EXERCISE
( ) TIME

MOOD
ANGRY/FRUSTRATED · SAD · TIRED · NUMB · HAPPY · EXCITED/FULFILLED

WHAT WENT RIGHT

WHAT DID I LEARN

FOR TOMORROW

TODAY'S Journal

DATE: / /

S M T W T F S

TODAY I'M GRATEFUL FOR:

1.
2.
3.

WATER INTAKE

1 2 3 4 5 6 7 8 (Glass)

EXERCISE

( ) TIME

MOOD

ANGRY/FRUSTRATED   SAD   TIRED   NUMB   HAPPY   EXCITED/FULFILLED

WHAT WENT RIGHT

WHAT DID I LEARN

FOR TOMORROW

TODAY'S Journal

DATE: / /

S M T W T F S

TODAY I'M GRATEFUL FOR:

1.
2.
3.

WATER INTAKE

1 2 3 4 5 6 7 8 (Glass)

EXERCISE

( ) TIME

MOOD

ANGRY/FRUSTRATED | SAD | TIRED | NUMB | HAPPY | EXCITED/FULFILLED

WHAT WENT RIGHT

WHAT DID I LEARN

FOR TOMORROW

NOTES:

NOTES:

WHAT DO I NEED TO PROCESS:

WEEKLY *Planner*

MONDAY

TUESDAY

WEDNESDAY

THURSDAY

FRIDAY

SATURDAY

SUNDAY

NOTES

TODAY'S Journal

DATE: / /

S M T W T F S

TODAY I'M GRATEFUL FOR:

1.
2.
3.

WATER INTAKE

1 2 3 4 5 6 7 8 (Glass)

EXERCISE

TIME

MOOD

ANGRY/FRUSTRATED SAD TIRED NUMB HAPPY EXCITED/FULFILLED

WHAT WENT RIGHT

WHAT DID I LEARN

FOR TOMORROW

TODAY'S Journal

DATE: /   /

S   M   T   W   T   F   S

TODAY I'M GRATEFUL FOR:

1.
2.
3.

WATER INTAKE

1   2   3   4   5   6   7   8   (Glass)

EXERCISE

(   ) TIME

MOOD

ANGRY/FRUSTRATED   SAD   TIRED   NUMB   HAPPY   EXCITED/FULFILLED

WHAT WENT RIGHT

WHAT DID I LEARN

FOR TOMORROW

TODAY'S *Journal*

DATE: / /

S M T W T F S

TODAY I'M GRATEFUL FOR:

1.
2.
3.

WATER INTAKE

1 2 3 4 5 6 7 8 (Glass)

EXERCISE

( ) TIME

MOOD

ANGRY/FRUSTRATED SAD TIRED NUMB HAPPY EXCITED/FULFILLED

WHAT WENT RIGHT

WHAT DID I LEARN

FOR TOMORROW

TODAY'S Journal

DATE: / /

☼ ☼ ☼ ☼ ☼ ☼ ☼
S M T W T F S

TODAY I'M GRATEFUL FOR:

1. _____
2. _____
3. _____

WATER INTAKE

💧 💧 💧 💧 💧 💧 💧 💧
1 2 3 4 5 6 7 8 (Glass)

EXERCISE

(_____)
TIME

MOOD

ANGRY/FRUSTRATED · SAD · TIRED · NUMB · HAPPY · EXCITED/FULFILLED

WHAT WENT RIGHT

_____
_____
_____
_____

WHAT DID I LEARN

_____
_____
_____

FOR TOMORROW

_____
_____
_____

TODAY'S Journal

DATE: /   /

S M T W T F S

TODAY I'M GRATEFUL FOR:

1. ....
2. ....
3. ....

WATER INTAKE

1 2 3 4 5 6 7 8 (Glass)

EXERCISE

( ) TIME

MOOD

ANGRY/FRUSTRATED   SAD   TIRED   NUMB   HAPPY   EXCITED/FULFILLED

WHAT WENT RIGHT

WHAT DID I LEARN

FOR TOMORROW

TODAY'S Journal

DATE: /   /

S M T W T F S

TODAY I'M GRATEFUL FOR:

1.
2.
3.

WATER INTAKE

1 2 3 4 5 6 7 8 (Glass)

EXERCISE

( ) TIME

MOOD

ANGRY/FRUSTRATED · SAD · TIRED · NUMB · HAPPY · EXCITED/FULFILLED

WHAT WENT RIGHT

WHAT DID I LEARN

FOR TOMORROW

TODAY'S
Journal

DATE: / /

S M T W T F S

TODAY I'M GRATEFUL FOR:

1.
2.
3.

WATER INTAKE

1 2 3 4 5 6 7 8 (Glass)

EXERCISE

( ) TIME

MOOD

ANGRY/FRUSTRATED   SAD   TIRED   NUMB   HAPPY   EXCITED/FULFILLED

WHAT WENT RIGHT

WHAT DID I LEARN

FOR TOMORROW

NOTES:

NOTES:

WHAT DO I NEED TO PROCESS:

WEEKLY *Planner*

MONDAY

TUESDAY

WEDNESDAY

THURSDAY

FRIDAY

SATURDAY

SUNDAY

NOTES

TODAY'S Journal

DATE: / /

S M T W T F S

TODAY I'M GRATEFUL FOR:

1. ....
2. ....
3. ....

WATER INTAKE

1 2 3 4 5 6 7 8 (Glass)

EXERCISE

( ) TIME

MOOD

ANGRY/FRUSTRATED SAD TIRED NUMB HAPPY EXCITED/FULFILLED

WHAT WENT RIGHT

....
....
....
....
....
....

WHAT DID I LEARN

....
....
....
....

FOR TOMORROW

....
....
....
....

TODAY'S *Journal*

DATE: / /

S M T W T F S

TODAY I'M GRATEFUL FOR:

1.
2.
3.

WATER INTAKE

1 2 3 4 5 6 7 8 (Glass)

EXERCISE

( ) TIME

MOOD

ANGRY/FRUSTRATED   SAD   TIRED   NUMB   HAPPY   EXCITED/FULFILLED

WHAT WENT RIGHT

WHAT DID I LEARN

FOR TOMORROW

TODAY'S
Journal

DATE: /   /

☀ ☀ ☀ ☀ ☀ ☀ ☀
S   M   T   W   T   F   S

TODAY I'M GRATEFUL FOR:

1. _____

2. _____

3. _____

WATER INTAKE

💧 💧 💧 💧 💧 💧 💧 💧
1   2   3   4   5   6   7   8   (Glass)

EXERCISE

(   ) TIME

MOOD

ANGRY/FRUSTRATED   SAD   TIRED   NUMB   HAPPY   EXCITED/FULFILLED

WHAT WENT RIGHT

_____
_____
_____
_____
_____

WHAT DID I LEARN

_____
_____
_____
_____

FOR TOMORROW

_____
_____
_____
_____

TODAY'S Journal

DATE: / /

S M T W T F S

TODAY I'M GRATEFUL FOR:

1.
2.
3.

WATER INTAKE

1 2 3 4 5 6 7 8 (Glass)

EXERCISE

( ) TIME

MOOD

ANGRY/FRUSTRATED   SAD   TIRED   NUMB   HAPPY   EXCITED/FULFILLED

WHAT WENT RIGHT

WHAT DID I LEARN

FOR TOMORROW

TODAY'S
Journal

DATE: / /

S M T W T F S

TODAY I'M GRATEFUL FOR:

1.
2.
3.

WATER INTAKE

1 2 3 4 5 6 7 8 (Glass)

EXERCISE

(TIME)

MOOD

ANGRY/FRUSTRATED SAD TIRED NUMB HAPPY EXCITED/FULFILLED

WHAT WENT RIGHT

WHAT DID I LEARN

FOR TOMORROW

TODAY'S Journal

DATE: /   /

S M T W T F S

TODAY I'M GRATEFUL FOR:

1. ....

2. ....

3. ....

WATER INTAKE

1 2 3 4 5 6 7 8 (Glass)

EXERCISE

(_____) TIME

MOOD

ANGRY/FRUSTRATED   SAD   TIRED   NUMB   HAPPY   EXCITED/FULFILLED

WHAT WENT RIGHT

WHAT DID I LEARN

FOR TOMORROW

TODAY'S Journal

DATE: / /

S M T W T F S

TODAY I'M GRATEFUL FOR:

1.
2.
3.

WATER INTAKE
1 2 3 4 5 6 7 8 (Glass)

EXERCISE
( ) TIME

MOOD
ANGRY/FRUSTRATED SAD TIRED NUMB HAPPY EXCITED/FULFILLED

WHAT WENT RIGHT

WHAT DID I LEARN

FOR TOMORROW

NOTES:

NOTES:

WHAT DO I NEED TO PROCESS:

WEEKLY Planner

MONDAY

TUESDAY

WEDNESDAY

THURSDAY

FRIDAY

SATURDAY

SUNDAY

NOTES

TODAY'S Journal

DATE: /   /

S M T W T F S

TODAY I'M GRATEFUL FOR:

1. ....
2. ....
3. ....

WATER INTAKE

1 2 3 4 5 6 7 8 (Glass)

EXERCISE

( ) TIME

MOOD

ANGRY/FRUSTRATED   SAD   TIRED   NUMB   HAPPY   EXCITED/FULFILLED

WHAT WENT RIGHT

WHAT DID I LEARN

FOR TOMORROW

TODAY'S
Journal

DATE: / /

S M T W T F S

TODAY I'M GRATEFUL FOR:

1.
2.
3.

WATER INTAKE

1 2 3 4 5 6 7 8 (Glass)

EXERCISE

( )
TIME

MOOD

ANGRY/FRUSTRATED   SAD   TIRED   NUMB   HAPPY   EXCITED/FULFILLED

WHAT WENT RIGHT

WHAT DID I LEARN

FOR TOMORROW

TODAY'S Journal

DATE: / /

S M T W T F S

TODAY I'M GRATEFUL FOR:

1. ....
2. ....
3. ....

WATER INTAKE

1 2 3 4 5 6 7 8 (Glass)

EXERCISE

( ) TIME

MOOD

ANGRY/FRUSTRATED   SAD   TIRED   NUMB   HAPPY   EXCITED/FULFILLED

WHAT WENT RIGHT

WHAT DID I LEARN

FOR TOMORROW

TODAY'S Journal

DATE: / /

S M T W T F S

TODAY I'M GRATEFUL FOR:

1.
2.
3.

WATER INTAKE

1 2 3 4 5 6 7 8 (Glass)

EXERCISE

( ) TIME

MOOD

ANGRY/FRUSTRATED SAD TIRED NUMB HAPPY EXCITED/FULFILLED

WHAT WENT RIGHT

WHAT DID I LEARN

FOR TOMORROW

TODAY'S
Journal

DATE: / /

S M T W T F S

TODAY I'M GRATEFUL FOR:

1. ....

2. ....

3. ....

WATER INTAKE

1 2 3 4 5 6 7 8 (Glass)

EXERCISE

( ) TIME

MOOD

ANGRY/FRUSTRATED   SAD   TIRED   NUMB   HAPPY   EXCITED/FULFILLED

WHAT WENT RIGHT

....
....
....
....
....
....

WHAT DID I LEARN

....
....
....
....

FOR TOMORROW

....
....
....
....

TODAY'S Journal

DATE: / /

S M T W T F S

TODAY I'M GRATEFUL FOR:

1.
2.
3.

WATER INTAKE

1 2 3 4 5 6 7 8 (Glass)

EXERCISE

( )
TIME

MOOD

ANGRY/FRUSTRATED   SAD   TIRED   NUMB   HAPPY   EXCITED/FULFILLED

WHAT WENT RIGHT

WHAT DID I LEARN

FOR TOMORROW

TODAY'S Journal

DATE: / /

☀ ☀ ☀ ☀ ☀ ☀ ☀
S M T W T F S

TODAY I'M GRATEFUL FOR:

1.
2.
3.

WATER INTAKE

💧 💧 💧 💧 💧 💧 💧 💧
1 2 3 4 5 6 7 8 (Glass)

EXERCISE

(   )
   TIME

MOOD

☹ ☹ 😑 😐 🙂 😂
ANGRY/ SAD TIRED NUMB HAPPY EXCITED/
FRUSTRATED   FULFILLED

WHAT WENT RIGHT

WHAT DID I LEARN

FOR TOMORROW

NOTES:

NOTES:

WHAT DO I NEED TO PROCESS:

WEEKLY *Planner*

MONDAY

TUESDAY

WEDNESDAY

THURSDAY

FRIDAY

SATURDAY

SUNDAY

NOTES

TODAY'S Journal

DATE: / /

S M T W T F S

TODAY I'M GRATEFUL FOR:

1.
2.
3.

WATER INTAKE

1 2 3 4 5 6 7 8 (Glass)

EXERCISE

( ) TIME

MOOD

ANGRY/FRUSTRATED   SAD   TIRED   NUMB   HAPPY   EXCITED/FULFILLED

WHAT WENT RIGHT

WHAT DID I LEARN

FOR TOMORROW

TODAY'S
Journal

DATE: / /

S M T W T F S

TODAY I'M GRATEFUL FOR:

1. ....
2. ....
3. ....

WATER INTAKE

1 2 3 4 5 6 7 8 (Glass)

EXERCISE

(_____)
TIME

MOOD

ANGRY/FRUSTRATED   SAD   TIRED   NUMB   HAPPY   EXCITED/FULFILLED

WHAT WENT RIGHT

WHAT DID I LEARN

FOR TOMORROW

TODAY'S Journal

DATE: / /

S M T W T F S

TODAY I'M GRATEFUL FOR:

1. ....
2. ....
3. ....

WATER INTAKE

1 2 3 4 5 6 7 8 (Glass)

EXERCISE

( ) TIME

MOOD

ANGRY/FRUSTRATED SAD TIRED NUMB HAPPY EXCITED/FULFILLED

WHAT WENT RIGHT

WHAT DID I LEARN

FOR TOMORROW

TODAY'S Journal

DATE: / /

S M T W T F S

TODAY I'M GRATEFUL FOR:

1.
2.
3.

WATER INTAKE

1 2 3 4 5 6 7 8 (Glass)

EXERCISE

( )
TIME

MOOD

ANGRY/FRUSTRATED · SAD · TIRED · NUMB · HAPPY · EXCITED/FULFILLED

WHAT WENT RIGHT

WHAT DID I LEARN

FOR TOMORROW

TODAY'S Journal

DATE: / /

S M T W T F S

TODAY I'M GRATEFUL FOR:

1.
2.
3.

WATER INTAKE

1 2 3 4 5 6 7 8 (Glass)

EXERCISE

( )
TIME

MOOD

ANGRY/FRUSTRATED   SAD   TIRED   NUMB   HAPPY   EXCITED/FULFILLED

WHAT WENT RIGHT

WHAT DID I LEARN

FOR TOMORROW

TODAY'S
Journal

DATE: / /

S M T W T F S

TODAY I'M GRATEFUL FOR:

1.
2.
3.

WATER INTAKE

1 2 3 4 5 6 7 8 (Glass)

EXERCISE

( )
TIME

MOOD

ANGRY/FRUSTRATED   SAD   TIRED   NUMB   HAPPY   EXCITED/FULFILLED

WHAT WENT RIGHT

WHAT DID I LEARN

FOR TOMORROW

TODAY'S Journal

DATE: / /

S M T W T F S

TODAY I'M GRATEFUL FOR:

1. ....
2. ....
3. ....

WATER INTAKE

1 2 3 4 5 6 7 8 (Glass)

EXERCISE

( ) TIME

MOOD

ANGRY/FRUSTRATED   SAD   TIRED   NUMB   HAPPY   EXCITED/FULFILLED

WHAT WENT RIGHT

WHAT DID I LEARN

FOR TOMORROW

NOTES:

NOTES:

WHAT DO I NEED TO PROCESS:

WEEKLY *Planner*

MONDAY

TUESDAY

WEDNESDAY

THURSDAY

FRIDAY

SATURDAY

SUNDAY

NOTES

TODAY'S Journal

DATE: / /

S M T W T F S

TODAY I'M GRATEFUL FOR:

1.
2.
3.

WATER INTAKE

1 2 3 4 5 6 7 8 (Glass)

EXERCISE

( ) TIME

MOOD

ANGRY/FRUSTRATED — SAD — TIRED — NUMB — HAPPY — EXCITED/FULFILLED

WHAT WENT RIGHT

WHAT DID I LEARN

FOR TOMORROW

TODAY'S Journal

DATE: /   /

S M T W T F S

TODAY I'M GRATEFUL FOR:

1. ....
2. ....
3. ....

WATER INTAKE

1 2 3 4 5 6 7 8 (Glass)

EXERCISE

(   ) TIME

MOOD

ANGRY/FRUSTRATED   SAD   TIRED   NUMB   HAPPY   EXCITED/FULFILLED

WHAT WENT RIGHT

....
....
....
....
....

WHAT DID I LEARN

....
....
....
....

FOR TOMORROW

....
....
....
....

TODAY'S Journal

DATE: / /

☼ ☼ ☼ ☼ ☼ ☼ ☼
S M T W T F S

TODAY I'M GRATEFUL FOR:

1. ....
2. ....
3. ....

WATER INTAKE

💧 💧 💧 💧 💧 💧 💧 💧
1 2 3 4 5 6 7 8 (Glass)

EXERCISE

( ) TIME

MOOD

| ANGRY/FRUSTRATED | SAD | TIRED | NUMB | HAPPY | EXCITED/FULFILLED |

WHAT WENT RIGHT

....
....
....
....

WHAT DID I LEARN

....
....
....
....

FOR TOMORROW

....
....
....
....

TODAY'S Journal

DATE: / /

S M T W T F S

TODAY I'M GRATEFUL FOR:

1.
2.
3.

WATER INTAKE

1 2 3 4 5 6 7 8 (Glass)

EXERCISE

( ) TIME

MOOD

ANGRY/FRUSTRATED   SAD   TIRED   NUMB   HAPPY   EXCITED/FULFILLED

WHAT WENT RIGHT

WHAT DID I LEARN

FOR TOMORROW

TODAY'S Journal

DATE: ___ / ___ / ___

S M T W T F S

TODAY I'M GRATEFUL FOR:

1. ....
2. ....
3. ....

WATER INTAKE

1 2 3 4 5 6 7 8 (Glass)

EXERCISE

(_____) TIME

MOOD

ANGRY/FRUSTRATED · SAD · TIRED · NUMB · HAPPY · EXCITED/FULFILLED

WHAT WENT RIGHT

....
....
....
....

WHAT DID I LEARN

....
....
....

FOR TOMORROW

....
....
....

TODAY'S *Journal*

DATE: / /

S M T W T F S

TODAY I'M GRATEFUL FOR:

1.
2.
3.

WATER INTAKE

1 2 3 4 5 6 7 8 (Glass)

EXERCISE

(TIME)

MOOD

ANGRY/FRUSTRATED   SAD   TIRED   NUMB   HAPPY   EXCITED/FULFILLED

WHAT WENT RIGHT

WHAT DID I LEARN

FOR TOMORROW

TODAY'S Journal

DATE: / /

S M T W T F S

TODAY I'M GRATEFUL FOR:

1.
2.
3.

WATER INTAKE

1 2 3 4 5 6 7 8 (Glass)

EXERCISE

TIME

MOOD

ANGRY/FRUSTRATED   SAD   TIRED   NUMB   HAPPY   EXCITED/FULFILLED

WHAT WENT RIGHT

WHAT DID I LEARN

FOR TOMORROW

NOTES:

NOTES:

WHAT DO I NEED TO PROCESS:

WEEKLY *Planner*

MONDAY

TUESDAY

WEDNESDAY

THURSDAY

FRIDAY

SATURDAY

SUNDAY

NOTES

TODAY'S
Journal

DATE: / /

S M T W T F S

TODAY I'M GRATEFUL FOR:

1.
2.
3.

WATER INTAKE

1 2 3 4 5 6 7 8 (Glass)

EXERCISE

( ) TIME

MOOD

ANGRY/FRUSTRATED   SAD   TIRED   NUMB   HAPPY   EXCITED/FULFILLED

WHAT WENT RIGHT

WHAT DID I LEARN

FOR TOMORROW

TODAY'S Journal

DATE: /   /

S M T W T F S

TODAY I'M GRATEFUL FOR:

1. ....

2. ....

3. ....

WATER INTAKE

1 2 3 4 5 6 7 8 (Glass)

EXERCISE

( )
TIME

MOOD

ANGRY/FRUSTRATED SAD TIRED NUMB HAPPY EXCITED/FULFILLED

WHAT WENT RIGHT

WHAT DID I LEARN

FOR TOMORROW

TODAY'S Journal

DATE: / /

S M T W T F S

TODAY I'M GRATEFUL FOR:

1. ....
2. ....
3. ....

WATER INTAKE

1 2 3 4 5 6 7 8 (Glass)

EXERCISE

( ) TIME

MOOD

ANGRY/FRUSTRATED   SAD   TIRED   NUMB   HAPPY   EXCITED/FULFILLED

WHAT WENT RIGHT

....
....
....
....
....

WHAT DID I LEARN

....
....
....
....

FOR TOMORROW

....
....
....
....

TODAY'S Journal

DATE: / /

S M T W T F S

TODAY I'M GRATEFUL FOR:

1. ....

2. ....

3. ....

WATER INTAKE

1 2 3 4 5 6 7 8 (Glass)

EXERCISE

( ) TIME

MOOD

ANGRY/FRUSTRATED   SAD   TIRED   NUMB   HAPPY   EXCITED/FULFILLED

WHAT WENT RIGHT

WHAT DID I LEARN

FOR TOMORROW

TODAY'S
Journal

DATE: / /

S M T W T F S

TODAY I'M GRATEFUL FOR:

1.
2.
3.

WATER INTAKE

1 2 3 4 5 6 7 8 (Glass)

EXERCISE

( ) TIME

MOOD

ANGRY/FRUSTRATED   SAD   TIRED   NUMB   HAPPY   EXCITED/FULFILLED

WHAT WENT RIGHT

WHAT DID I LEARN

FOR TOMORROW

TODAY'S Journal

DATE: / /

S M T W T F S

TODAY I'M GRATEFUL FOR:

1.
2.
3.

WATER INTAKE

1 2 3 4 5 6 7 8 (Glass)

EXERCISE

( ) TIME

MOOD

ANGRY/FRUSTRATED SAD TIRED NUMB HAPPY EXCITED/FULFILLED

WHAT WENT RIGHT

WHAT DID I LEARN

FOR TOMORROW

TODAY'S
Journal

DATE: / /

S M T W T F S

TODAY I'M GRATEFUL FOR:

1. _____
2. _____
3. _____

WATER INTAKE

1 2 3 4 5 6 7 8 (Glass)

EXERCISE

(___) TIME

MOOD

ANGRY/FRUSTRATED   SAD   TIRED   NUMB   HAPPY   EXCITED/FULFILLED

WHAT WENT RIGHT

_____
_____
_____
_____
_____

WHAT DID I LEARN

_____
_____
_____
_____

FOR TOMORROW

_____
_____
_____
_____

NOTES:

NOTES:

WHAT DO I NEED TO PROCESS:

WEEKLY *Planner*

MONDAY

TUESDAY

WEDNESDAY

THURSDAY

FRIDAY

SATURDAY

SUNDAY

NOTES

TODAY'S
Journal

DATE: ___ / ___ / ___

☀ ☀ ☀ ☀ ☀ ☀ ☀
S M T W T F S

TODAY I'M GRATEFUL FOR:

1. ....
2. ....
3. ....

WATER INTAKE
💧 💧 💧 💧 💧 💧 💧 💧
1   2   3   4   5   6   7   8   (Glass)

EXERCISE
🏋 🏃 ⚽ 🧘 🥋 (   )
TIME

MOOD
😠   😟   😌   😐   🙂   😂
ANGRY/   SAD   TIRED   NUMB   HAPPY   EXCITED/
FRUSTRATED   FULFILLED

WHAT WENT RIGHT

....
....
....
....
....

WHAT DID I LEARN

....
....
....
....

FOR TOMORROW

....
....
....
....

TODAY'S
Journal

DATE: /   /

☼ ☼ ☼ ☼ ☼ ☼ ☼
S   M   T   W   T   F   S

TODAY I'M GRATEFUL FOR:

1. ....

2. ....

3. ....

WATER INTAKE

💧 💧 💧 💧 💧 💧 💧 💧
1   2   3   4   5   6   7   8   (Glass)

EXERCISE

(   )
TIME

MOOD

😠   🙁   😌   😐   🙂   😂
ANGRY/ SAD TIRED NUMB HAPPY EXCITED/
FRUSTRATED   FULFILLED

WHAT WENT RIGHT

....

....

....

....

WHAT DID I LEARN

....

....

....

....

FOR TOMORROW

....

....

....

....

TODAY'S Journal

DATE: / /

S M T W T F S

TODAY I'M GRATEFUL FOR:

1.
2.
3.

WATER INTAKE

1 2 3 4 5 6 7 8 (Glass)

EXERCISE

( ) TIME

MOOD

ANGRY/FRUSTRATED SAD TIRED NUMB HAPPY EXCITED/FULFILLED

WHAT WENT RIGHT

WHAT DID I LEARN

FOR TOMORROW

TODAY'S Journal

DATE: / /

S M T W T F S

TODAY I'M GRATEFUL FOR:

1.
2.
3.

WATER INTAKE

1 2 3 4 5 6 7 8 (Glass)

EXERCISE

( ) TIME

MOOD

ANGRY/FRUSTRATED · SAD · TIRED · NUMB · HAPPY · EXCITED/FULFILLED

WHAT WENT RIGHT

WHAT DID I LEARN

FOR TOMORROW

TODAY'S
Journal

DATE: /   /

S M T W T F S

TODAY I'M GRATEFUL FOR:

1.
2.
3.

WATER INTAKE
1 2 3 4 5 6 7 8 (Glass)

EXERCISE
(   ) TIME

MOOD
ANGRY/FRUSTRATED   SAD   TIRED   NUMB   HAPPY   EXCITED/FULFILLED

WHAT WENT RIGHT

WHAT DID I LEARN

FOR TOMORROW

TODAY'S Journal

DATE: / /

S M T W T F S

TODAY I'M GRATEFUL FOR:

1. ....

2. ....

3. ....

WATER INTAKE
1 2 3 4 5 6 7 8 (Glass)

EXERCISE
( )
TIME

MOOD
ANGRY/FRUSTRATED   SAD   TIRED   NUMB   HAPPY   EXCITED/FULFILLED

WHAT WENT RIGHT

....
....
....
....

WHAT DID I LEARN

....
....
....
....

FOR TOMORROW

....
....
....
....

TODAY'S Journal

DATE: / /

S M T W T F S

TODAY I'M GRATEFUL FOR:

1. ....
2. ....
3. ....

WATER INTAKE

1 2 3 4 5 6 7 8 (Glass)

EXERCISE

( )
TIME

MOOD

ANGRY/FRUSTRATED   SAD   TIRED   NUMB   HAPPY   EXCITED/FULFILLED

WHAT WENT RIGHT

WHAT DID I LEARN

FOR TOMORROW

NOTES:

NOTES:

WHAT DO I NEED TO PROCESS:

WEEKLY *Planner*

MONDAY

TUESDAY

WEDNESDAY

THURSDAY

FRIDAY

SATURDAY

SUNDAY

NOTES

TODAY'S
Journal

DATE: / /

S M T W T F S

TODAY I'M GRATEFUL FOR:

1. ....
2. ....
3. ....

WATER INTAKE

1 2 3 4 5 6 7 8 (Glass)

EXERCISE

( ) TIME

MOOD

ANGRY/FRUSTRATED | SAD | TIRED | NUMB | HAPPY | EXCITED/FULFILLED

WHAT WENT RIGHT

....
....
....
....
....
....

WHAT DID I LEARN

....
....
....
....

FOR TOMORROW

....
....
....
....

TODAY'S Journal

DATE: / /

S M T W T F S

TODAY I'M GRATEFUL FOR:

1. ....

2. ....

3. ....

WATER INTAKE

1 2 3 4 5 6 7 8 (Glass)

EXERCISE

( ) TIME

MOOD

ANGRY/FRUSTRATED · SAD · TIRED · NUMB · HAPPY · EXCITED/FULFILLED

WHAT WENT RIGHT

WHAT DID I LEARN

FOR TOMORROW

TODAY'S
Journal

DATE: / /

S M T W T F S

TODAY I'M GRATEFUL FOR:

1. ....

2. ....

3. ....

WATER INTAKE

1 2 3 4 5 6 7 8 (Glass)

EXERCISE

( ) TIME

MOOD

ANGRY/FRUSTRATED SAD TIRED NUMB HAPPY EXCITED/FULFILLED

WHAT WENT RIGHT

WHAT DID I LEARN

FOR TOMORROW

TODAY'S Journal

DATE: / /

S M T W T F S

TODAY I'M GRATEFUL FOR:

1.
2.
3.

WATER INTAKE

1 2 3 4 5 6 7 8 (Glass)

EXERCISE

( )
TIME

MOOD

ANGRY/FRUSTRATED   SAD   TIRED   NUMB   HAPPY   EXCITED/FULFILLED

WHAT WENT RIGHT

WHAT DID I LEARN

FOR TOMORROW

TODAY'S *Journal*

DATE: __ / __ / __

S M T W T F S

TODAY I'M GRATEFUL FOR:

1. ....
2. ....
3. ....

WATER INTAKE

1 2 3 4 5 6 7 8 (Glass)

EXERCISE

( ) TIME

MOOD

ANGRY/FRUSTRATED   SAD   TIRED   NUMB   HAPPY   EXCITED/FULFILLED

WHAT WENT RIGHT

WHAT DID I LEARN

FOR TOMORROW

TODAY'S
Journal

DATE: / /

S M T W T F S

TODAY I'M GRATEFUL FOR:

1.
2.
3.

WATER INTAKE

1 2 3 4 5 6 7 8 (Glass)

EXERCISE

( )
TIME

MOOD

ANGRY/FRUSTRATED SAD TIRED NUMB HAPPY EXCITED/FULFILLED

WHAT WENT RIGHT

WHAT DID I LEARN

FOR TOMORROW

TODAY'S
Journal

DATE: /   /

S M T W T F S

TODAY I'M GRATEFUL FOR:

1. ....

2. ....

3. ....

WATER INTAKE

1 2 3 4 5 6 7 8 (Glass)

EXERCISE

( ) TIME

MOOD

ANGRY/FRUSTRATED   SAD   TIRED   NUMB   HAPPY   EXCITED/FULFILLED

WHAT WENT RIGHT

WHAT DID I LEARN

FOR TOMORROW

NOTES:

NOTES:

WHAT DO I NEED TO PROCESS:

WEEKLY *Planner*

MONDAY

TUESDAY

WEDNESDAY

THURSDAY

FRIDAY

SATURDAY

SUNDAY

NOTES

TODAY'S Journal

DATE: / /

S M T W T F S

TODAY I'M GRATEFUL FOR:

1.
2.
3.

WATER INTAKE

1 2 3 4 5 6 7 8 (Glass)

EXERCISE

( ) TIME

MOOD

ANGRY/FRUSTRATED · SAD · TIRED · NUMB · HAPPY · EXCITED/FULFILLED

WHAT WENT RIGHT

WHAT DID I LEARN

FOR TOMORROW

TODAY'S Journal

DATE: / /

S M T W T F S

TODAY I'M GRATEFUL FOR:

1.

2.

3.

WATER INTAKE

1 2 3 4 5 6 7 8 (Glass)

EXERCISE

( ) TIME

MOOD

ANGRY/FRUSTRATED   SAD   TIRED   NUMB   HAPPY   EXCITED/FULFILLED

WHAT WENT RIGHT

WHAT DID I LEARN

FOR TOMORROW

TODAY'S *Journal*

DATE: ___ / ___ / ___

☀ ☀ ☀ ☀ ☀ ☀ ☀
S M T W T F S

TODAY I'M GRATEFUL FOR:

1. ....
2. ....
3. ....

WATER INTAKE

💧 💧 💧 💧 💧 💧 💧 💧
1 2 3 4 5 6 7 8 (Glass)

EXERCISE

(   ) TIME

MOOD

ANGRY/FRUSTRATED   SAD   TIRED   NUMB   HAPPY   EXCITED/FULFILLED

WHAT WENT RIGHT

....
....
....
....

WHAT DID I LEARN

....
....
....

FOR TOMORROW

....
....
....

TODAY'S Journal

DATE: / /

S M T W T F S

TODAY I'M GRATEFUL FOR:

1.
2.
3.

WATER INTAKE

1 2 3 4 5 6 7 8 (Glass)

EXERCISE

( ) TIME

MOOD

ANGRY/FRUSTRATED   SAD   TIRED   NUMB   HAPPY   EXCITED/FULFILLED

WHAT WENT RIGHT

WHAT DID I LEARN

FOR TOMORROW

TODAY'S Journal

DATE: /   /

S   M   T   W   T   F   S

TODAY I'M GRATEFUL FOR:

1.
2.
3.

WATER INTAKE

1   2   3   4   5   6   7   8   (Glass)

EXERCISE

(   ) TIME

MOOD

ANGRY/FRUSTRATED   SAD   TIRED   NUMB   HAPPY   EXCITED/FULFILLED

WHAT WENT RIGHT

WHAT DID I LEARN

FOR TOMORROW

TODAY'S Journal

DATE: / /

S M T W T F S

TODAY I'M GRATEFUL FOR:

1.

2.

3.

WATER INTAKE

1 2 3 4 5 6 7 8 (Glass)

EXERCISE

( )
TIME

MOOD

ANGRY/FRUSTRATED   SAD   TIRED   NUMB   HAPPY   EXCITED/FULFILLED

WHAT WENT RIGHT

WHAT DID I LEARN

FOR TOMORROW

TODAY'S
Journal

DATE: / /

S M T W T F S

TODAY I'M GRATEFUL FOR:

1. ....
2. ....
3. ....

WATER INTAKE
1 2 3 4 5 6 7 8 (Glass)

EXERCISE
( ) TIME

MOOD
ANGRY/FRUSTRATED · SAD · TIRED · NUMB · HAPPY · EXCITED/FULFILLED

WHAT WENT RIGHT

WHAT DID I LEARN

FOR TOMORROW

NOTES:

NOTES:

WHAT DO I NEED TO PROCESS:

WEEKLY *Planner*

MONDAY

TUESDAY

WEDNESDAY

THURSDAY

FRIDAY

SATURDAY

SUNDAY

NOTES

TODAY'S Journal

DATE: ___ / ___ / ___

☀ ☀ ☀ ☀ ☀ ☀ ☀
S M T W T F S

TODAY I'M GRATEFUL FOR:

1. _____

2. _____

3. _____

WATER INTAKE

💧 💧 💧 💧 💧 💧 💧 💧
1 2 3 4 5 6 7 8 (Glass)

EXERCISE

(   ) TIME

MOOD

ANGRY/FRUSTRATED   SAD   TIRED   NUMB   HAPPY   EXCITED/FULFILLED

WHAT WENT RIGHT

_____
_____
_____
_____
_____

WHAT DID I LEARN

_____
_____
_____

FOR TOMORROW

_____
_____
_____

TODAY'S Journal

DATE: / /

S M T W T F S

TODAY I'M GRATEFUL FOR:

1.
2.
3.

WATER INTAKE

1 2 3 4 5 6 7 8 (Glass)

EXERCISE

( ) TIME

MOOD

ANGRY/FRUSTRATED   SAD   TIRED   NUMB   HAPPY   EXCITED/FULFILLED

WHAT WENT RIGHT

WHAT DID I LEARN

FOR TOMORROW

TODAY'S *Journal*

DATE: __ / __ / __

S M T W T F S

TODAY I'M GRATEFUL FOR:

1. ....
2. ....
3. ....

WATER INTAKE

1 2 3 4 5 6 7 8 (Glass)

EXERCISE

(_____) TIME

MOOD

ANGRY/FRUSTRATED SAD TIRED NUMB HAPPY EXCITED/FULFILLED

WHAT WENT RIGHT

....
....
....
....
....

WHAT DID I LEARN

....
....
....
....

FOR TOMORROW

....
....
....
....

TODAY'S Journal

DATE: /   /

☼ ☼ ☼ ☼ ☼ ☼ ☼
S M T W T F S

TODAY I'M GRATEFUL FOR:

1. ....

2. ....

3. ....

WATER INTAKE

💧 💧 💧 💧 💧 💧 💧 💧
1 2 3 4 5 6 7 8 (Glass)

EXERCISE

(   )
         TIME

MOOD

😠   😟   😑   😐   🙂   😂
ANGRY/   SAD   TIRED   NUMB   HAPPY   EXCITED/
FRUSTRATED   FULFILLED

WHAT WENT RIGHT

....
....
....
....
....
....

WHAT DID I LEARN

....
....
....
....
....

FOR TOMORROW

....
....
....
....
....

TODAY'S
Journal

DATE: / /

S M T W T F S

TODAY I'M GRATEFUL FOR:

1. ....
2. ....
3. ....

WATER INTAKE

1 2 3 4 5 6 7 8 (Glass)

EXERCISE

(   ) TIME

MOOD

ANGRY/FRUSTRATED SAD TIRED NUMB HAPPY EXCITED/FULFILLED

WHAT WENT RIGHT

....
....
....
....

WHAT DID I LEARN

....
....
....
....

FOR TOMORROW

....
....
....
....

TODAY'S
Journal

DATE: /   /

S M T W T F S

TODAY I'M GRATEFUL FOR:

1. ....

2. ....

3. ....

WATER INTAKE

1   2   3   4   5   6   7   8   (Glass)

EXERCISE

( ) TIME

MOOD

ANGRY/FRUSTRATED   SAD   TIRED   NUMB   HAPPY   EXCITED/FULFILLED

WHAT WENT RIGHT

....
....
....
....

WHAT DID I LEARN

....
....
....
....

FOR TOMORROW

....
....
....
....

TODAY'S
Journal

DATE: / /

S M T W T F S

TODAY I'M GRATEFUL FOR:

1. ....

2. ....

3. ....

WATER INTAKE

1 2 3 4 5 6 7 8 (Glass)

EXERCISE

( ) TIME

MOOD

ANGRY/FRUSTRATED   SAD   TIRED   NUMB   HAPPY   EXCITED/FULFILLED

WHAT WENT RIGHT

....

....

....

....

WHAT DID I LEARN

....

....

....

....

FOR TOMORROW

....

....

....

....

NOTES:

NOTES:

WHAT DO I NEED TO PROCESS:

WEEKLY *Planner*

MONDAY

TUESDAY

WEDNESDAY

THURSDAY

FRIDAY

SATURDAY

SUNDAY

NOTES

TODAY'S
Journal

DATE: /   /

S   M   T   W   T   F   S

TODAY I'M GRATEFUL FOR:

1.
2.
3.

WATER INTAKE

1   2   3   4   5   6   7   8   (Glass)

EXERCISE

(   ) TIME

MOOD

ANGRY/FRUSTRATED   SAD   TIRED   NUMB   HAPPY   EXCITED/FULFILLED

WHAT WENT RIGHT

WHAT DID I LEARN

FOR TOMORROW

TODAY'S Journal

DATE: / /

S M T W T F S

TODAY I'M GRATEFUL FOR:

1.
2.
3.

WATER INTAKE

1 2 3 4 5 6 7 8 (Glass)

EXERCISE

( )
TIME

MOOD

ANGRY/FRUSTRATED SAD TIRED NUMB HAPPY EXCITED/FULFILLED

WHAT WENT RIGHT

WHAT DID I LEARN

FOR TOMORROW

TODAY'S Journal

DATE: / /

S M T W T F S

TODAY I'M GRATEFUL FOR:

1.
2.
3.

WATER INTAKE

1 2 3 4 5 6 7 8 (Glass)

EXERCISE

( ) TIME

MOOD

ANGRY/FRUSTRATED   SAD   TIRED   NUMB   HAPPY   EXCITED/FULFILLED

WHAT WENT RIGHT

WHAT DID I LEARN

FOR TOMORROW

TODAY'S Journal

DATE: / /

S M T W T F S

TODAY I'M GRATEFUL FOR:

1.
2.
3.

WATER INTAKE

1 2 3 4 5 6 7 8 (Glass)

EXERCISE

( ) TIME

MOOD

ANGRY/FRUSTRATED SAD TIRED NUMB HAPPY EXCITED/FULFILLED

WHAT WENT RIGHT

WHAT DID I LEARN

FOR TOMORROW

TODAY'S Journal

DATE: /   /

S M T W T F S

TODAY I'M GRATEFUL FOR:

1.
2.
3.

WATER INTAKE

1 2 3 4 5 6 7 8 (Glass)

EXERCISE

(   ) TIME

MOOD

ANGRY/FRUSTRATED   SAD   TIRED   NUMB   HAPPY   EXCITED/FULFILLED

WHAT WENT RIGHT

WHAT DID I LEARN

FOR TOMORROW

TODAY'S Journal

DATE: / /

S M T W T F S

TODAY I'M GRATEFUL FOR:

1.

2.

3.

WATER INTAKE

1 2 3 4 5 6 7 8 (Glass)

EXERCISE

( ) TIME

MOOD

ANGRY/FRUSTRATED   SAD   TIRED   NUMB   HAPPY   EXCITED/FULFILLED

WHAT WENT RIGHT

WHAT DID I LEARN

FOR TOMORROW

TODAY'S Journal

DATE: / /

S M T W T F S

TODAY I'M GRATEFUL FOR:

1.

2.

3.

WATER INTAKE

1 2 3 4 5 6 7 8 (Glass)

EXERCISE

( ) TIME

MOOD

ANGRY/FRUSTRATED   SAD   TIRED   NUMB   HAPPY   EXCITED/FULFILLED

WHAT WENT RIGHT

WHAT DID I LEARN

FOR TOMORROW

NOTES:

NOTES:

WHAT DO I NEED TO PROCESS:

WEEKLY *Planner*

MONDAY

TUESDAY

WEDNESDAY

THURSDAY

FRIDAY

SATURDAY

SUNDAY

NOTES

TODAY'S Journal

DATE: / /

S M T W T F S

TODAY I'M GRATEFUL FOR:

1.
2.
3.

WATER INTAKE

1 2 3 4 5 6 7 8 (Glass)

EXERCISE

( ) TIME

MOOD

ANGRY/FRUSTRATED SAD TIRED NUMB HAPPY EXCITED/FULFILLED

WHAT WENT RIGHT

WHAT DID I LEARN

FOR TOMORROW

TODAY'S Journal

DATE: / /

S M T W T F S

TODAY I'M GRATEFUL FOR:

1.
2.
3.

WATER INTAKE

1 2 3 4 5 6 7 8 (Glass)

EXERCISE

( )
TIME

MOOD

ANGRY/FRUSTRATED   SAD   TIRED   NUMB   HAPPY   EXCITED/FULFILLED

WHAT WENT RIGHT

WHAT DID I LEARN

FOR TOMORROW

TODAY'S
Journal

DATE: /   /

S M T W T F S

TODAY I'M GRATEFUL FOR:

1. ....

2. ....

3. ....

WATER INTAKE

1 2 3 4 5 6 7 8 (Glass)

EXERCISE

(   ) TIME

MOOD

ANGRY/FRUSTRATED　SAD　TIRED　NUMB　HAPPY　EXCITED/FULFILLED

WHAT WENT RIGHT

WHAT DID I LEARN

FOR TOMORROW

TODAY'S *Journal*

DATE: /   /

☀ ☀ ☀ ☀ ☀ ☀ ☀
S M T W T F S

TODAY I'M GRATEFUL FOR:

1. ....

2. ....

3. ....

WATER INTAKE

💧 💧 💧 💧 💧 💧 💧 💧
1   2   3   4   5   6   7   8   (Glass)

EXERCISE

(   )
TIME

MOOD

😠 ☹ 😌 😐 🙂 😆
ANGRY/   SAD   TIRED   NUMB   HAPPY   EXCITED/
FRUSTRATED   FULFILLED

WHAT WENT RIGHT

....

....

....

....

....

WHAT DID I LEARN

....

....

....

....

FOR TOMORROW

....

....

....

....

TODAY'S Journal

DATE: / /

S M T W T F S

TODAY I'M GRATEFUL FOR:

1.
2.
3.

WATER INTAKE

1 2 3 4 5 6 7 8 (Glass)

EXERCISE

( ) TIME

MOOD

ANGRY/FRUSTRATED   SAD   TIRED   NUMB   HAPPY   EXCITED/FULFILLED

WHAT WENT RIGHT

WHAT DID I LEARN

FOR TOMORROW

TODAY'S Journal

DATE: / /

S M T W T F S

TODAY I'M GRATEFUL FOR:

1. ....

2. ....

3. ....

WATER INTAKE

1 2 3 4 5 6 7 8 (Glass)

EXERCISE

( )
TIME

MOOD

ANGRY/FRUSTRATED   SAD   TIRED   NUMB   HAPPY   EXCITED/FULFILLED

WHAT WENT RIGHT

....
....
....
....
....

WHAT DID I LEARN

....
....
....
....

FOR TOMORROW

....
....
....
....

TODAY'S Journal

DATE: / /

S M T W T F S

TODAY I'M GRATEFUL FOR:

1.
2.
3.

WATER INTAKE

1 2 3 4 5 6 7 8 (Glass)

EXERCISE

( ) TIME

MOOD

ANGRY/FRUSTRATED · SAD · TIRED · NUMB · HAPPY · EXCITED/FULFILLED

WHAT WENT RIGHT

WHAT DID I LEARN

FOR TOMORROW

NOTES:

NOTES:

WHAT DO I NEED TO PROCESS:

WEEKLY Planner

MONDAY

TUESDAY

WEDNESDAY

THURSDAY

FRIDAY

SATURDAY

SUNDAY

NOTES

TODAY'S Journal

DATE: /   /

S M T W T F S

TODAY I'M GRATEFUL FOR:

1.
2.
3.

WATER INTAKE

1 2 3 4 5 6 7 8 (Glass)

EXERCISE

( ) TIME

MOOD

ANGRY/FRUSTRATED   SAD   TIRED   NUMB   HAPPY   EXCITED/FULFILLED

WHAT WENT RIGHT

WHAT DID I LEARN

FOR TOMORROW

TODAY'S Journal

DATE: / /

S M T W T F S

TODAY I'M GRATEFUL FOR:

1.
2.
3.

WATER INTAKE

1 2 3 4 5 6 7 8 (Glass)

EXERCISE

( )
TIME

MOOD

ANGRY/FRUSTRATED   SAD   TIRED   NUMB   HAPPY   EXCITED/FULFILLED

WHAT WENT RIGHT

WHAT DID I LEARN

FOR TOMORROW

TODAY'S *Journal*

DATE: /   /

S M T W T F S

TODAY I'M GRATEFUL FOR:

1. _____

2. _____

3. _____

WATER INTAKE

1 2 3 4 5 6 7 8 (Glass)

EXERCISE

(   ) TIME

MOOD

ANGRY/FRUSTRATED SAD TIRED NUMB HAPPY EXCITED/FULFILLED

WHAT WENT RIGHT

_____
_____
_____
_____
_____

WHAT DID I LEARN

_____
_____
_____
_____

FOR TOMORROW

_____
_____
_____
_____

TODAY'S Journal

DATE: /   /

S M T W T F S

TODAY I'M GRATEFUL FOR:

1.
2.
3.

WATER INTAKE

1 2 3 4 5 6 7 8 (Glass)

EXERCISE

( )
TIME

MOOD

ANGRY/FRUSTRATED   SAD   TIRED   NUMB   HAPPY   EXCITED/FULFILLED

WHAT WENT RIGHT

WHAT DID I LEARN

FOR TOMORROW

TODAY'S Journal

DATE: / /

S M T W T F S

TODAY I'M GRATEFUL FOR:

1.

2.

3.

WATER INTAKE

1 2 3 4 5 6 7 8 (Glass)

EXERCISE

( ) TIME

MOOD

ANGRY/FRUSTRATED SAD TIRED NUMB HAPPY EXCITED/FULFILLED

WHAT WENT RIGHT

WHAT DID I LEARN

FOR TOMORROW

TODAY'S Journal

DATE: / /

S M T W T F S

TODAY I'M GRATEFUL FOR:

1.

2.

3.

WATER INTAKE

1 2 3 4 5 6 7 8 (Glass)

EXERCISE

( )
TIME

MOOD

ANGRY/FRUSTRATED   SAD   TIRED   NUMB   HAPPY   EXCITED/FULFILLED

WHAT WENT RIGHT

WHAT DID I LEARN

FOR TOMORROW

TODAY'S *Journal*

DATE: ___ / ___ / ___

S M T W T F S

TODAY I'M GRATEFUL FOR:

1. _____

2. _____

3. _____

WATER INTAKE

1 2 3 4 5 6 7 8 (Glass)

EXERCISE

(_____) TIME

MOOD

ANGRY/FRUSTRATED   SAD   TIRED   NUMB   HAPPY   EXCITED/FULFILLED

WHAT WENT RIGHT

_____
_____
_____
_____
_____

WHAT DID I LEARN

_____
_____
_____
_____

FOR TOMORROW

_____
_____
_____
_____

NOTES:

NOTES:

WHAT DO I NEED TO PROCESS:

WEEKLY *Planner*

MONDAY

TUESDAY

WEDNESDAY

THURSDAY

FRIDAY

SATURDAY

SUNDAY

NOTES

TODAY'S Journal

DATE: / /

S M T W T F S

TODAY I'M GRATEFUL FOR:

1.
2.
3.

WATER INTAKE

1 2 3 4 5 6 7 8 (Glass)

EXERCISE

( )
TIME

MOOD

ANGRY/FRUSTRATED   SAD   TIRED   NUMB   HAPPY   EXCITED/FULFILLED

WHAT WENT RIGHT

WHAT DID I LEARN

FOR TOMORROW

TODAY'S
Journal

DATE: / /

S M T W T F S

TODAY I'M GRATEFUL FOR:

1. _____
2. _____
3. _____

WATER INTAKE
1 2 3 4 5 6 7 8 (Glass)

EXERCISE
( ) TIME

MOOD
ANGRY/FRUSTRATED   SAD   TIRED   NUMB   HAPPY   EXCITED/FULFILLED

WHAT WENT RIGHT

WHAT DID I LEARN

FOR TOMORROW

TODAY'S Journal

DATE: / /

S M T W T F S

TODAY I'M GRATEFUL FOR:

1.
2.
3.

WATER INTAKE

1 2 3 4 5 6 7 8 (Glass)

EXERCISE

( ) TIME

MOOD

ANGRY/FRUSTRATED   SAD   TIRED   NUMB   HAPPY   EXCITED/FULFILLED

WHAT WENT RIGHT

WHAT DID I LEARN

FOR TOMORROW

TODAY'S Journal

DATE: / /

☼ ☼ ☼ ☼ ☼ ☼ ☼
S M T W T F S

TODAY I'M GRATEFUL FOR:

1. _____
2. _____
3. _____

WATER INTAKE
1 2 3 4 5 6 7 8 (Glass)

EXERCISE
( ) TIME

MOOD
ANGRY/FRUSTRATED SAD TIRED NUMB HAPPY EXCITED/FULFILLED

WHAT WENT RIGHT

_____
_____
_____
_____
_____

WHAT DID I LEARN

_____
_____
_____
_____

FOR TOMORROW

_____
_____
_____
_____

TODAY'S Journal

DATE: / /

S M T W T F S

TODAY I'M GRATEFUL FOR:

1. ....
2. ....
3. ....

WATER INTAKE

1 2 3 4 5 6 7 8 (Glass)

EXERCISE

( ) TIME

MOOD

ANGRY/FRUSTRATED SAD TIRED NUMB HAPPY EXCITED/FULFILLED

WHAT WENT RIGHT

....
....
....
....
....

WHAT DID I LEARN

....
....
....
....

FOR TOMORROW

....
....
....
....

TODAY'S Journal

DATE: / /

S M T W T F S

TODAY I'M GRATEFUL FOR:

1.
2.
3.

WATER INTAKE

1 2 3 4 5 6 7 8 (Glass)

EXERCISE

( )
TIME

MOOD

ANGRY/FRUSTRATED   SAD   TIRED   NUMB   HAPPY   EXCITED/FULFILLED

WHAT WENT RIGHT

WHAT DID I LEARN

FOR TOMORROW

TODAY'S
Journal

DATE: / /

S M T W T F S

TODAY I'M GRATEFUL FOR:

1.
2.
3.

WATER INTAKE

1 2 3 4 5 6 7 8 (Glass)

EXERCISE

( ) TIME

MOOD

ANGRY/FRUSTRATED SAD TIRED NUMB HAPPY EXCITED/FULFILLED

WHAT WENT RIGHT

WHAT DID I LEARN

FOR TOMORROW

NOTES:

NOTES:

WHAT DO I NEED TO PROCESS:

WEEKLY *Planner*

MONDAY

TUESDAY

WEDNESDAY

THURSDAY

FRIDAY

SATURDAY

SUNDAY

NOTES

TODAY'S Journal

DATE: / /

S M T W T F S

TODAY I'M GRATEFUL FOR:

1.
2.
3.

WATER INTAKE

1 2 3 4 5 6 7 8 (Glass)

EXERCISE

( ) TIME

MOOD

ANGRY/FRUSTRATED SAD TIRED NUMB HAPPY EXCITED/FULFILLED

WHAT WENT RIGHT

WHAT DID I LEARN

FOR TOMORROW

TODAY'S Journal

DATE: / /

S M T W T F S

TODAY I'M GRATEFUL FOR:

1.
2.
3.

WATER INTAKE

1 2 3 4 5 6 7 8 (Glass)

EXERCISE

( )
TIME

MOOD

ANGRY/FRUSTRATED SAD TIRED NUMB HAPPY EXCITED/FULFILLED

WHAT WENT RIGHT

WHAT DID I LEARN

FOR TOMORROW

TODAY'S Journal

DATE: / /

S M T W T F S

TODAY I'M GRATEFUL FOR:

1.
2.
3.

WATER INTAKE

1 2 3 4 5 6 7 8 (Glass)

EXERCISE

( ) TIME

MOOD

ANGRY/FRUSTRATED   SAD   TIRED   NUMB   HAPPY   EXCITED/FULFILLED

WHAT WENT RIGHT

WHAT DID I LEARN

FOR TOMORROW

TODAY'S
Journal

DATE: / /

S M T W T F S

TODAY I'M GRATEFUL FOR:

1.
2.
3.

WATER INTAKE

1 2 3 4 5 6 7 8 (Glass)

EXERCISE

( ) TIME

MOOD

ANGRY/FRUSTRATED · SAD · TIRED · NUMB · HAPPY · EXCITED/FULFILLED

WHAT WENT RIGHT

WHAT DID I LEARN

FOR TOMORROW

TODAY'S Journal

DATE: / /

S M T W T F S

TODAY I'M GRATEFUL FOR:

1.
2.
3.

WATER INTAKE

1 2 3 4 5 6 7 8 (Glass)

EXERCISE

( ) TIME

MOOD

ANGRY/FRUSTRATED SAD TIRED NUMB HAPPY EXCITED/FULFILLED

WHAT WENT RIGHT

WHAT DID I LEARN

FOR TOMORROW

TODAY'S Journal

DATE: / /

S M T W T F S

TODAY I'M GRATEFUL FOR:

1.

2.

3.

WATER INTAKE

1 2 3 4 5 6 7 8 (Glass)

EXERCISE

( ) TIME

MOOD

ANGRY/FRUSTRATED   SAD   TIRED   NUMB   HAPPY   EXCITED/FULFILLED

WHAT WENT RIGHT

WHAT DID I LEARN

FOR TOMORROW

TODAY'S
Journal

DATE: /   /

S M T W T F S

TODAY I'M GRATEFUL FOR:

1. _____

2. _____

3. _____

WATER INTAKE

1 2 3 4 5 6 7 8 (Glass)

EXERCISE

(___) TIME

MOOD

ANGRY/FRUSTRATED   SAD   TIRED   NUMB   HAPPY   EXCITED/FULFILLED

WHAT WENT RIGHT

_____
_____
_____
_____
_____

WHAT DID I LEARN

_____
_____
_____

FOR TOMORROW

_____
_____
_____

NOTES:

NOTES:

WHAT DO I NEED TO PROCESS:

WEEKLY *Planner*

MONDAY

TUESDAY

WEDNESDAY

THURSDAY

FRIDAY

SATURDAY

SUNDAY

NOTES

TODAY'S
Journal

DATE: / /

S M T W T F S

TODAY I'M GRATEFUL FOR:

1.
2.
3.

WATER INTAKE

1 2 3 4 5 6 7 8 (Glass)

EXERCISE

( ) TIME

MOOD

ANGRY/FRUSTRATED   SAD   TIRED   NUMB   HAPPY   EXCITED/FULFILLED

WHAT WENT RIGHT

WHAT DID I LEARN

FOR TOMORROW

TODAY'S Journal

DATE: / /

S M T W T F S

TODAY I'M GRATEFUL FOR:

1. ....
2. ....
3. ....

WATER INTAKE

1 2 3 4 5 6 7 8 (Glass)

EXERCISE

(____) TIME

MOOD

ANGRY/FRUSTRATED SAD TIRED NUMB HAPPY EXCITED/FULFILLED

WHAT WENT RIGHT

....
....
....
....
....

WHAT DID I LEARN

....
....
....
....

FOR TOMORROW

....
....
....
....

TODAY'S Journal

DATE: / /

S M T W T F S

TODAY I'M GRATEFUL FOR:

1.
2.
3.

WATER INTAKE

1 2 3 4 5 6 7 8 (Glass)

EXERCISE

( ) TIME

MOOD

ANGRY/FRUSTRATED   SAD   TIRED   NUMB   HAPPY   EXCITED/FULFILLED

WHAT WENT RIGHT

WHAT DID I LEARN

FOR TOMORROW

TODAY'S Journal

DATE: / /

S M T W T F S

TODAY I'M GRATEFUL FOR:

1.
2.
3.

WATER INTAKE

1 2 3 4 5 6 7 8 (Glass)

EXERCISE

( )
TIME

MOOD

ANGRY/FRUSTRATED   SAD   TIRED   NUMB   HAPPY   EXCITED/FULFILLED

WHAT WENT RIGHT

WHAT DID I LEARN

FOR TOMORROW

TODAY'S Journal

DATE: / /

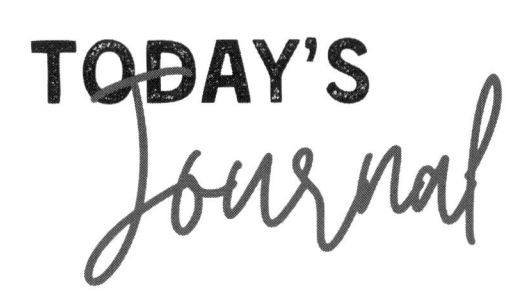

S M T W T F S

TODAY I'M GRATEFUL FOR:

1.

2.

3.

WATER INTAKE

1 2 3 4 5 6 7 8 (Glass)

EXERCISE

( ) TIME

MOOD

ANGRY/FRUSTRATED SAD TIRED NUMB HAPPY EXCITED/FULFILLED

WHAT WENT RIGHT

WHAT DID I LEARN

FOR TOMORROW

TODAY'S Journal

DATE: / /

S M T W T F S

TODAY I'M GRATEFUL FOR:

1.
2.
3.

WATER INTAKE

1 2 3 4 5 6 7 8 (Glass)

EXERCISE

( )
TIME

MOOD

ANGRY/FRUSTRATED   SAD   TIRED   NUMB   HAPPY   EXCITED/FULFILLED

WHAT WENT RIGHT

WHAT DID I LEARN

FOR TOMORROW

TODAY'S
Journal

DATE: / /

S M T W T F S

TODAY I'M GRATEFUL FOR:

1.
2.
3.

WATER INTAKE

1 2 3 4 5 6 7 8 (Glass)

EXERCISE

( ) TIME

MOOD

ANGRY/FRUSTRATED   SAD   TIRED   NUMB   HAPPY   EXCITED/FULFILLED

WHAT WENT RIGHT

WHAT DID I LEARN

FOR TOMORROW

NOTES:

NOTES:

WHAT DO I NEED TO PROCESS:

WEEKLY Planner

MONDAY

TUESDAY

WEDNESDAY

THURSDAY

FRIDAY

SATURDAY

SUNDAY

NOTES

TODAY'S Journal

DATE: / /

S M T W T F S

TODAY I'M GRATEFUL FOR:

1.
2.
3.

WATER INTAKE

1 2 3 4 5 6 7 8 (Glass)

EXERCISE

( ) TIME

MOOD

ANGRY/FRUSTRATED   SAD   TIRED   NUMB   HAPPY   EXCITED/FULFILLED

WHAT WENT RIGHT

WHAT DID I LEARN

FOR TOMORROW

TODAY'S Journal

DATE: / /

S M T W T F S

TODAY I'M GRATEFUL FOR:

1.
2.
3.

WATER INTAKE

1 2 3 4 5 6 7 8 (Glass)

EXERCISE

( ) TIME

MOOD

ANGRY/FRUSTRATED   SAD   TIRED   NUMB   HAPPY   EXCITED/FULFILLED

WHAT WENT RIGHT

WHAT DID I LEARN

FOR TOMORROW

TODAY'S Journal

DATE: / /

S M T W T F S

TODAY I'M GRATEFUL FOR:

1.
2.
3.

WATER INTAKE

1 2 3 4 5 6 7 8 (Glass)

EXERCISE

( ) TIME

MOOD

ANGRY/FRUSTRATED   SAD   TIRED   NUMB   HAPPY   EXCITED/FULFILLED

WHAT WENT RIGHT

WHAT DID I LEARN

FOR TOMORROW

TODAY'S Journal

DATE: / /

S M T W T F S

TODAY I'M GRATEFUL FOR:

1.
2.
3.

WATER INTAKE

1 2 3 4 5 6 7 8 (Glass)

EXERCISE

( ) TIME

MOOD

ANGRY/FRUSTRATED | SAD | TIRED | NUMB | HAPPY | EXCITED/FULFILLED

WHAT WENT RIGHT

WHAT DID I LEARN

FOR TOMORROW

TODAY'S Journal

DATE: / /

S M T W T F S

TODAY I'M GRATEFUL FOR:

1.
2.
3.

WATER INTAKE

1 2 3 4 5 6 7 8 (Glass)

EXERCISE

( ) TIME

MOOD

ANGRY/FRUSTRATED   SAD   TIRED   NUMB   HAPPY   EXCITED/FULFILLED

WHAT WENT RIGHT

WHAT DID I LEARN

FOR TOMORROW

TODAY'S Journal

DATE: / /

S M T W T F S

TODAY I'M GRATEFUL FOR:

1.
2.
3.

WATER INTAKE

1 2 3 4 5 6 7 8 (Glass)

EXERCISE

( ) TIME

MOOD

ANGRY/FRUSTRATED SAD TIRED NUMB HAPPY EXCITED/FULFILLED

WHAT WENT RIGHT

WHAT DID I LEARN

FOR TOMORROW

TODAY'S
Journal

DATE: / /

S M T W T F S

TODAY I'M GRATEFUL FOR:

1.
2.
3.

WATER INTAKE

1 2 3 4 5 6 7 8 (Glass)

EXERCISE

( ) TIME

MOOD

ANGRY/FRUSTRATED   SAD   TIRED   NUMB   HAPPY   EXCITED/FULFILLED

WHAT WENT RIGHT

WHAT DID I LEARN

FOR TOMORROW

NOTES:

NOTES:

WHAT DO I NEED TO PROCESS:

WEEKLY *Planner*

MONDAY

TUESDAY

WEDNESDAY

THURSDAY

FRIDAY

SATURDAY

SUNDAY

NOTES

TODAY'S Journal

DATE: / /

S M T W T F S

TODAY I'M GRATEFUL FOR:

1.
2.
3.

WATER INTAKE

1 2 3 4 5 6 7 8 (Glass)

EXERCISE

( ) TIME

MOOD

ANGRY/FRUSTRATED — SAD — TIRED — NUMB — HAPPY — EXCITED/FULFILLED

WHAT WENT RIGHT

WHAT DID I LEARN

FOR TOMORROW

TODAY'S Journal

DATE: / /

S M T W T F S

TODAY I'M GRATEFUL FOR:

1.
2.
3.

WATER INTAKE

1 2 3 4 5 6 7 8 (Glass)

EXERCISE

( )
TIME

MOOD

ANGRY/FRUSTRATED   SAD   TIRED   NUMB   HAPPY   EXCITED/FULFILLED

WHAT WENT RIGHT

WHAT DID I LEARN

FOR TOMORROW

TODAY'S
Journal

DATE: / /

S M T W T F S

TODAY I'M GRATEFUL FOR:

1.
2.
3.

WATER INTAKE

1 2 3 4 5 6 7 8 (Glass)

EXERCISE

(   )
TIME

MOOD

ANGRY/FRUSTRATED SAD TIRED NUMB HAPPY EXCITED/FULFILLED

WHAT WENT RIGHT

WHAT DID I LEARN

FOR TOMORROW

TODAY'S Journal

DATE: / /

S M T W T F S

TODAY I'M GRATEFUL FOR:

1.
2.
3.

WATER INTAKE

1 2 3 4 5 6 7 8 (Glass)

EXERCISE

( )
TIME

MOOD

ANGRY/FRUSTRATED SAD TIRED NUMB HAPPY EXCITED/FULFILLED

WHAT WENT RIGHT

WHAT DID I LEARN

FOR TOMORROW

TODAY'S
Journal

DATE: / /

S M T W T F S

TODAY I'M GRATEFUL FOR:

1.
2.
3.

WATER INTAKE

1 2 3 4 5 6 7 8 (Glass)

EXERCISE

( ) TIME

MOOD

ANGRY/FRUSTRATED · SAD · TIRED · NUMB · HAPPY · EXCITED/FULFILLED

WHAT WENT RIGHT

WHAT DID I LEARN

FOR TOMORROW

TODAY'S Journal

DATE: /   /

☼ ☼ ☼ ☼ ☼ ☼ ☼
S M T W T F S

TODAY I'M GRATEFUL FOR:

1. ....

2. ....

3. ....

WATER INTAKE

💧 💧 💧 💧 💧 💧 💧 💧
1 2 3 4 5 6 7 8 (Glass)

EXERCISE

(   )
      TIME

MOOD

ANGRY/   SAD   TIRED   NUMB   HAPPY   EXCITED/
FRUSTRATED   FULFILLED

WHAT WENT RIGHT

....
....
....
....

WHAT DID I LEARN

....
....
....
....

FOR TOMORROW

....
....
....
....

TODAY'S Journal

DATE: / /

S M T W T F S

TODAY I'M GRATEFUL FOR:

1.
2.
3.

WATER INTAKE

1 2 3 4 5 6 7 8 (Glass)

EXERCISE

( ) TIME

MOOD

ANGRY/FRUSTRATED   SAD   TIRED   NUMB   HAPPY   EXCITED/FULFILLED

WHAT WENT RIGHT

WHAT DID I LEARN

FOR TOMORROW

NOTES:

NOTES:

WHAT DO I NEED TO PROCESS:

WEEKLY *Planner*

MONDAY

TUESDAY

WEDNESDAY

THURSDAY

FRIDAY

SATURDAY

SUNDAY

NOTES

TODAY'S
Journal

DATE: / /

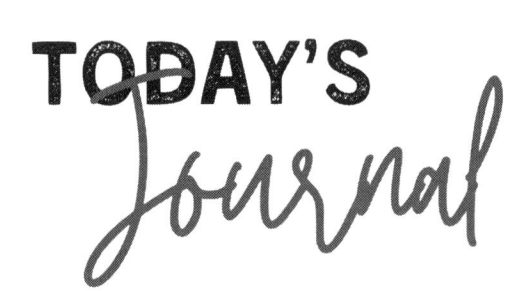

S M T W T F S

TODAY I'M GRATEFUL FOR:

1.
2.
3.

WATER INTAKE
1 2 3 4 5 6 7 8 (Glass)

EXERCISE
( ) TIME

MOOD
ANGRY/FRUSTRATED · SAD · TIRED · NUMB · HAPPY · EXCITED/FULFILLED

WHAT WENT RIGHT

WHAT DID I LEARN

FOR TOMORROW

TODAY'S Journal

DATE: / /

S M T W T F S

TODAY I'M GRATEFUL FOR:

1.

2.

3.

WATER INTAKE

1 2 3 4 5 6 7 8 (Glass)

EXERCISE

( ) TIME

MOOD

ANGRY/FRUSTRATED · SAD · TIRED · NUMB · HAPPY · EXCITED/FULFILLED

WHAT WENT RIGHT

WHAT DID I LEARN

FOR TOMORROW

TODAY'S *Journal*

DATE: /   /

S M T W T F S

TODAY I'M GRATEFUL FOR:

1.
2.
3.

WATER INTAKE

1 2 3 4 5 6 7 8 (Glass)

EXERCISE

( ) TIME

MOOD

ANGRY/FRUSTRATED · SAD · TIRED · NUMB · HAPPY · EXCITED/FULFILLED

WHAT WENT RIGHT

WHAT DID I LEARN

FOR TOMORROW

TODAY'S
Journal

DATE: /   /

☼ ☼ ☼ ☼ ☼ ☼ ☼
S M T W T F S

TODAY I'M GRATEFUL FOR:

1.
2.
3.

WATER INTAKE

💧 💧 💧 💧 💧 💧 💧 💧
1 2 3 4 5 6 7 8 (Glass)

EXERCISE

(   )
         TIME

MOOD

ANGRY/   SAD   TIRED   NUMB   HAPPY   EXCITED/
FRUSTRATED   FULFILLED

WHAT WENT RIGHT

WHAT DID I LEARN

FOR TOMORROW

TODAY'S
Journal

DATE: / /

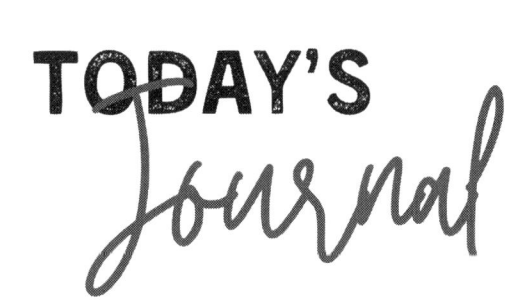

S M T W T F S

TODAY I'M GRATEFUL FOR:

1. _____
2. _____
3. _____

WATER INTAKE

1 2 3 4 5 6 7 8 (Glass)

EXERCISE

( ) TIME

MOOD

ANGRY/FRUSTRATED · SAD · TIRED · NUMB · HAPPY · EXCITED/FULFILLED

WHAT WENT RIGHT

WHAT DID I LEARN

FOR TOMORROW

TODAY'S Journal

DATE: / /

S M T W T F S

TODAY I'M GRATEFUL FOR:

1. _____

2. _____

3. _____

WATER INTAKE

1 2 3 4 5 6 7 8 (Glass)

EXERCISE

(____) TIME

MOOD

ANGRY/FRUSTRATED SAD TIRED NUMB HAPPY EXCITED/FULFILLED

WHAT WENT RIGHT

_____
_____
_____
_____
_____

WHAT DID I LEARN

_____
_____
_____
_____

FOR TOMORROW

_____
_____
_____
_____

TODAY'S Journal

DATE: /   /

S M T W T F S

TODAY I'M GRATEFUL FOR:

1.
2.
3.

WATER INTAKE

1 2 3 4 5 6 7 8   (Glass)

EXERCISE

(   ) TIME

MOOD

ANGRY/FRUSTRATED · SAD · TIRED · NUMB · HAPPY · EXCITED/FULFILLED

WHAT WENT RIGHT

WHAT DID I LEARN

FOR TOMORROW

NOTES:

NOTES:

WHAT DO I NEED TO PROCESS:

WEEKLY *Planner*

MONDAY

TUESDAY

WEDNESDAY

THURSDAY

FRIDAY

SATURDAY

SUNDAY

NOTES

TODAY'S Journal

DATE: / /

S M T W T F S

TODAY I'M GRATEFUL FOR:

1. _____
2. _____
3. _____

WATER INTAKE

1 2 3 4 5 6 7 8 (Glass)

EXERCISE

( ) TIME

MOOD

ANGRY/FRUSTRATED · SAD · TIRED · NUMB · HAPPY · EXCITED/FULFILLED

WHAT WENT RIGHT

WHAT DID I LEARN

FOR TOMORROW

TODAY'S
Journal

DATE: /   /

S M T W T F S

TODAY I'M GRATEFUL FOR:

1.
2.
3.

WATER INTAKE

1 2 3 4 5 6 7 8 (Glass)

EXERCISE

( ) TIME

MOOD

ANGRY/FRUSTRATED   SAD   TIRED   NUMB   HAPPY   EXCITED/FULFILLED

WHAT WENT RIGHT

WHAT DID I LEARN

FOR TOMORROW

TODAY'S
Journal

DATE: / /

S M T W T F S

TODAY I'M GRATEFUL FOR:

1.
2.
3.

WATER INTAKE

1 2 3 4 5 6 7 8 (Glass)

EXERCISE

( ) TIME

MOOD

ANGRY/FRUSTRATED   SAD   TIRED   NUMB   HAPPY   EXCITED/FULFILLED

WHAT WENT RIGHT

WHAT DID I LEARN

FOR TOMORROW

TODAY'S Journal

DATE: / /

S M T W T F S

TODAY I'M GRATEFUL FOR:

1.

2.

3.

WATER INTAKE

1 2 3 4 5 6 7 8 (Glass)

EXERCISE

( )
TIME

MOOD

ANGRY/FRUSTRATED   SAD   TIRED   NUMB   HAPPY   EXCITED/FULFILLED

WHAT WENT RIGHT

WHAT DID I LEARN

FOR TOMORROW

TODAY'S Journal

DATE: / /

S M T W T F S

TODAY I'M GRATEFUL FOR:

1.
2.
3.

WATER INTAKE

1 2 3 4 5 6 7 8 (Glass)

EXERCISE

(TIME)

MOOD

ANGRY/FRUSTRATED   SAD   TIRED   NUMB   HAPPY   EXCITED/FULFILLED

WHAT WENT RIGHT

WHAT DID I LEARN

FOR TOMORROW

TODAY'S Journal

DATE: / /

S M T W T F S

TODAY I'M GRATEFUL FOR:

1. ....
2. ....
3. ....

WATER INTAKE

1 2 3 4 5 6 7 8 (Glass)

EXERCISE

( ) TIME

MOOD

ANGRY/FRUSTRATED | SAD | TIRED | NUMB | HAPPY | EXCITED/FULFILLED

WHAT WENT RIGHT

WHAT DID I LEARN

FOR TOMORROW

TODAY'S *Journal*

DATE: /   /

S M T W T F S

TODAY I'M GRATEFUL FOR:

1. _____
2. _____
3. _____

WATER INTAKE

1 2 3 4 5 6 7 8 (Glass)

EXERCISE

(   ) TIME

MOOD

ANGRY/FRUSTRATED   SAD   TIRED   NUMB   HAPPY   EXCITED/FULFILLED

WHAT WENT RIGHT

_____
_____
_____
_____
_____

WHAT DID I LEARN

_____
_____
_____
_____

FOR TOMORROW

_____
_____
_____
_____

NOTES:

NOTES:

WHAT DO I NEED TO PROCESS:

WEEKLY *Planner*

MONDAY

TUESDAY

WEDNESDAY

THURSDAY

FRIDAY

SATURDAY

SUNDAY

NOTES

TODAY'S Journal

DATE: / /

S M T W T F S

TODAY I'M GRATEFUL FOR:

1. _____
2. _____
3. _____

WATER INTAKE

1 2 3 4 5 6 7 8 (Glass)

EXERCISE

( ) TIME

MOOD

ANGRY/FRUSTRATED · SAD · TIRED · NUMB · HAPPY · EXCITED/FULFILLED

WHAT WENT RIGHT

_____
_____
_____
_____

WHAT DID I LEARN

_____
_____
_____

FOR TOMORROW

_____
_____
_____

TODAY'S
Journal

DATE: /   /

S M T W T F S

TODAY I'M GRATEFUL FOR:

1.
2.
3.

WATER INTAKE

1 2 3 4 5 6 7 8 (Glass)

EXERCISE

( )
TIME

MOOD

ANGRY/FRUSTRATED   SAD   TIRED   NUMB   HAPPY   EXCITED/FULFILLED

WHAT WENT RIGHT

WHAT DID I LEARN

FOR TOMORROW

TODAY'S
Journal

DATE: ___ / ___ / ___

S M T W T F S

TODAY I'M GRATEFUL FOR:

1. _____
2. _____
3. _____

WATER INTAKE

1 2 3 4 5 6 7 8 (Glass)

EXERCISE

(___) TIME

MOOD

ANGRY/FRUSTRATED SAD TIRED NUMB HAPPY EXCITED/FULFILLED

WHAT WENT RIGHT

WHAT DID I LEARN

FOR TOMORROW

TODAY'S Journal

DATE: /   /

S M T W T F S

TODAY I'M GRATEFUL FOR:

1.

2.

3.

WATER INTAKE

1 2 3 4 5 6 7 8 (Glass)

EXERCISE

( ) TIME

MOOD

ANGRY/FRUSTRATED   SAD   TIRED   NUMB   HAPPY   EXCITED/FULFILLED

WHAT WENT RIGHT

WHAT DID I LEARN

FOR TOMORROW

TODAY'S
Journal

DATE: / /

S M T W T F S

TODAY I'M GRATEFUL FOR:

1.
2.
3.

WATER INTAKE

1 2 3 4 5 6 7 8 (Glass)

EXERCISE

( ) TIME

MOOD

ANGRY/FRUSTRATED   SAD   TIRED   NUMB   HAPPY   EXCITED/FULFILLED

WHAT WENT RIGHT

WHAT DID I LEARN

FOR TOMORROW

TODAY'S Journal

DATE: / /

S M T W T F S

TODAY I'M GRATEFUL FOR:

1.

2.

3.

WATER INTAKE

1 2 3 4 5 6 7 8 (Glass)

EXERCISE

( ) TIME

WHAT WENT RIGHT

MOOD

ANGRY/FRUSTRATED SAD TIRED NUMB HAPPY EXCITED/FULFILLED

WHAT DID I LEARN

FOR TOMORROW

TODAY'S
Journal

DATE: /   /

S   M   T   W   T   F   S

TODAY I'M GRATEFUL FOR:

1. ....
2. ....
3. ....

WATER INTAKE

1   2   3   4   5   6   7   8   (Glass)

EXERCISE

(   ) TIME

MOOD

ANGRY/FRUSTRATED   SAD   TIRED   NUMB   HAPPY   EXCITED/FULFILLED

WHAT WENT RIGHT

WHAT DID I LEARN

FOR TOMORROW

NOTES:

NOTES:

WHAT DO I NEED TO PROCESS:

WEEKLY *Planner*

MONDAY

TUESDAY

WEDNESDAY

THURSDAY

FRIDAY

SATURDAY

SUNDAY

NOTES

TODAY'S
Journal

DATE: / /

S M T W T F S

TODAY I'M GRATEFUL FOR:

1.
2.
3.

WATER INTAKE

1 2 3 4 5 6 7 8 (Glass)

EXERCISE

( ) TIME

MOOD

ANGRY/FRUSTRATED   SAD   TIRED   NUMB   HAPPY   EXCITED/FULFILLED

WHAT WENT RIGHT

WHAT DID I LEARN

FOR TOMORROW

TODAY'S Journal

DATE: / /

S M T W T F S

TODAY I'M GRATEFUL FOR:

1. ....

2. ....

3. ....

WATER INTAKE

1 2 3 4 5 6 7 8 (Glass)

EXERCISE

( ) TIME

MOOD

ANGRY/FRUSTRATED SAD TIRED NUMB HAPPY EXCITED/FULFILLED

WHAT WENT RIGHT

WHAT DID I LEARN

FOR TOMORROW

TODAY'S
Journal

DATE: / /

S M T W T F S

TODAY I'M GRATEFUL FOR:

1. ....
2. ....
3. ....

WATER INTAKE

1 2 3 4 5 6 7 8 (Glass)

EXERCISE

(   ) TIME

MOOD

ANGRY/FRUSTRATED   SAD   TIRED   NUMB   HAPPY   EXCITED/FULFILLED

WHAT WENT RIGHT

WHAT DID I LEARN

FOR TOMORROW

TODAY'S
Journal

DATE: / /

☼ ☼ ☼ ☼ ☼ ☼ ☼
S M T W T F S

TODAY I'M GRATEFUL FOR:

1. _____

2. _____

3. _____

WATER INTAKE

💧 💧 💧 💧 💧 💧 💧 💧
1 2 3 4 5 6 7 8 (Glass)

EXERCISE

🏋 🏃 🚶 🧘 🥋 ( ) TIME

MOOD

☹ ☹ 😔 😐 🙂 😆
ANGRY/   SAD   TIRED NUMB HAPPY EXCITED/
FRUSTRATED   FULFILLED

WHAT WENT RIGHT

_____
_____
_____
_____
_____

WHAT DID I LEARN

_____
_____
_____
_____
_____

FOR TOMORROW

_____
_____
_____
_____
_____

TODAY'S Journal

DATE: / /

S M T W T F S

TODAY I'M GRATEFUL FOR:

1.

2.

3.

WATER INTAKE

1 2 3 4 5 6 7 8 (Glass)

EXERCISE

( ) TIME

MOOD

ANGRY/FRUSTRATED — SAD — TIRED — NUMB — HAPPY — EXCITED/FULFILLED

WHAT WENT RIGHT

WHAT DID I LEARN

FOR TOMORROW

TODAY'S Journal

DATE: / /

S M T W T F S

TODAY I'M GRATEFUL FOR:

1.
2.
3.

WATER INTAKE

1 2 3 4 5 6 7 8 (Glass)

EXERCISE

( )
TIME

MOOD

ANGRY/ FRUSTRATED   SAD   TIRED   NUMB   HAPPY   EXCITED/ FULFILLED

WHAT WENT RIGHT

WHAT DID I LEARN

FOR TOMORROW

TODAY'S
Journal

DATE: / /

S M T W T F S

TODAY I'M GRATEFUL FOR:

1.

2.

3.

WATER INTAKE

1 2 3 4 5 6 7 8 (Glass)

EXERCISE

( ) TIME

MOOD

ANGRY/FRUSTRATED   SAD   TIRED   NUMB   HAPPY   EXCITED/FULFILLED

WHAT WENT RIGHT

WHAT DID I LEARN

FOR TOMORROW

NOTES:

NOTES:

WHAT DO I NEED TO PROCESS:

WEEKLY *Planner*

MONDAY

TUESDAY

WEDNESDAY

THURSDAY

FRIDAY

SATURDAY

SUNDAY

NOTES

TODAY'S Journal

DATE: __ / __ / __

S M T W T F S

TODAY I'M GRATEFUL FOR:

1. _____
2. _____
3. _____

WATER INTAKE

1 2 3 4 5 6 7 8 (Glass)

EXERCISE

(_____) TIME

MOOD

ANGRY/FRUSTRATED · SAD · TIRED · NUMB · HAPPY · EXCITED/FULFILLED

WHAT WENT RIGHT

_____
_____
_____
_____

WHAT DID I LEARN

_____
_____
_____
_____

FOR TOMORROW

_____
_____
_____
_____

TODAY'S Journal

DATE: /   /

S M T W T F S

TODAY I'M GRATEFUL FOR:

1.
2.
3.

WATER INTAKE

1 2 3 4 5 6 7 8 (Glass)

EXERCISE

( ) TIME

MOOD

ANGRY/FRUSTRATED   SAD   TIRED   NUMB   HAPPY   EXCITED/FULFILLED

WHAT WENT RIGHT

WHAT DID I LEARN

FOR TOMORROW

TODAY'S Journal

DATE: / /

S M T W T F S

TODAY I'M GRATEFUL FOR:

1.
2.
3.

WATER INTAKE

1 2 3 4 5 6 7 8 (Glass)

EXERCISE

( ) TIME

MOOD

ANGRY/FRUSTRATED   SAD   TIRED   NUMB   HAPPY   EXCITED/FULFILLED

WHAT WENT RIGHT

WHAT DID I LEARN

FOR TOMORROW

TODAY'S Journal

DATE: / /

☼ ☼ ☼ ☼ ☼ ☼ ☼
S M T W T F S

TODAY I'M GRATEFUL FOR:

1. ....

2. ....

3. ....

WATER INTAKE

💧 💧 💧 💧 💧 💧 💧 💧
1 2 3 4 5 6 7 8 (Glass)

EXERCISE

( ) TIME

MOOD

ANGRY/FRUSTRATED — SAD — TIRED — NUMB — HAPPY — EXCITED/FULFILLED

WHAT WENT RIGHT

....
....
....
....
....

WHAT DID I LEARN

....
....
....
....

FOR TOMORROW

....
....
....
....

TODAY'S
Journal

DATE: / /

S M T W T F S

TODAY I'M GRATEFUL FOR:

1.

2.

3.

WATER INTAKE

1 2 3 4 5 6 7 8 (Glass)

EXERCISE

( ) TIME

MOOD

ANGRY/FRUSTRATED   SAD   TIRED   NUMB   HAPPY   EXCITED/FULFILLED

WHAT WENT RIGHT

WHAT DID I LEARN

FOR TOMORROW

TODAY'S Journal

DATE: / /

S M T W T F S

TODAY I'M GRATEFUL FOR:

1.
2.
3.

WATER INTAKE

1 2 3 4 5 6 7 8 (Glass)

EXERCISE

( )
TIME

MOOD

ANGRY/FRUSTRATED SAD TIRED NUMB HAPPY EXCITED/FULFILLED

WHAT WENT RIGHT

WHAT DID I LEARN

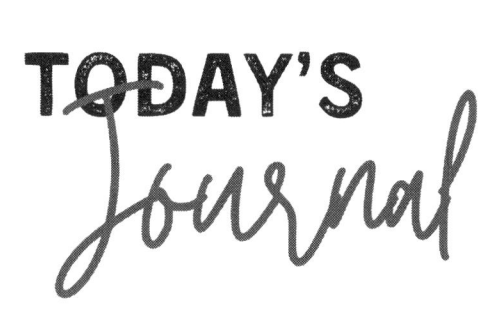

FOR TOMORROW

TODAY'S Journal

DATE: / /

S M T W T F S

TODAY I'M GRATEFUL FOR:

1.

2.

3.

WATER INTAKE

1 2 3 4 5 6 7 8 (Glass)

EXERCISE

( ) TIME

MOOD

ANGRY/FRUSTRATED SAD TIRED NUMB HAPPY EXCITED/FULFILLED

WHAT WENT RIGHT

WHAT DID I LEARN

FOR TOMORROW

NOTES:

NOTES:

WHAT DO I NEED TO PROCESS:

A Look Back

As you turn to this page, take a moment to reflect on the journey you've embarked upon. This space is dedicated to capturing the highlights of your mindfulness practice, the milestones in your resilience, and the evolution of your daily habits. It's a place to acknowledge your progress, contemplate the lessons learned, and appreciate the strides you've made in caring for your mental and physical health. Whether it's a breakthrough moment of clarity, a day when you felt particularly strong, or a habit that's become a cornerstone of your routine, jot it down here. Let these notes serve as a beacon of your dedication and a reminder of how far you've come. This is your story of growth and perseverance—celebrate each victory, big or small, and look back on them with pride.

A Look Forward

As you journey through the pages of this journal, you are not just recording your past, but also shaping your future. This section, "A Look Forward," is your canvas to paint your aspirations, set new goals, and establish intentions for your ongoing journey. This is a space for you to envision the next steps in your mindfulness practice, resilience building, and habit formation. It's a place to set your sights on what you want to achieve, and to plan how you'll get there. Whether it's a new fitness goal, a dietary change, or a mental health objective, write it down here.

Use this framework to guide your goal-setting process. Consider also the power of intention. Unlike goals, intentions are not attached to expected outcomes. They influence your approach to situations and decisions, keeping you focused on your purpose.

As you write, visualize your success. Picture yourself achieving these goals and living out these intentions. This visualization can serve as a powerful motivator on your journey. This is your space to dream, to plan, and to commit to your future self. As you continue your daily journaling, let this page be a guidepost, a reminder of where you're headed. This is your story of growth and perseverance—embrace the journey ahead with anticipation and resolve. These notes can be transferred to your next DAILY JOURNAL to help you continue on your path to a more fulfilled life.

Made in the USA
Columbia, SC
16 April 2024

edec2643-09c0-44c7-ad0a-f118f70e3dc9R01